FREE Test Taking Tips DVD Offer

To help us better serve you, we have developed a Test Taking Tips DVD that we would like to give you for FREE. **This DVD covers world-class test taking tips that you can use to be even more successful when you are taking your test.**

All that we ask is that you email us your feedback about your study guide. Please let us know what you thought about it – whether that is good, bad or indifferent.

To get your **FREE Test Taking Tips DVD**, email freedvd@studyguideteam.com with "FREE DVD" in the subject line and the following information in the body of the email:

      a. The title of your study guide.

      b. Your product rating on a scale of 1-5, with 5 being the highest rating.

      c. Your feedback about the study guide. What did you think of it?

      d. Your full name and shipping address to send your free DVD.

If you have any questions or concerns, please don't hesitate to contact us at freedvd@studyguideteam.com.

Thanks again!

Praxis Teaching Reading 5203 Elementary Education Study Guide

Praxis II Teaching Reading 5203
Test Prep & Practice Test Questions

Test Prep Books

Table of Contents

Quick Overview

As you draw closer to taking your exam, effective preparation becomes more and more important. Thankfully, you have this study guide to help you get ready. Use this guide to help keep your studying on track and refer to it often.

This study guide contains several key sections that will help you be successful on your exam. The guide contains tips for what you should do the night before and the day of the test. Also included are test-taking tips. Knowing the right information is not always enough. Many well-prepared test takers struggle with exams. These tips will help equip you to accurately read, assess, and answer test questions.

A large part of the guide is devoted to showing you what content to expect on the exam and to helping you better understand that content. In this guide are practice test questions so that you can see how well you have grasped the content. Then, answer explanations are provided so that you can understand why you missed certain questions.

Don't try to cram the night before you take your exam. This is not a wise strategy for a few reasons. First, your retention of the information will be low. Your time would be better used by reviewing information you already know rather than trying to learn a lot of new information. Second, you will likely become stressed as you try to gain a large amount of knowledge in a short amount of time. Third, you will be depriving yourself of sleep. So be sure to go to bed at a reasonable time the night before. Being well-rested helps you focus and remain calm.

Be sure to eat a substantial breakfast the morning of the exam. If you are taking the exam in the afternoon, be sure to have a good lunch as well. Being hungry is distracting and can make it difficult to focus. You have hopefully spent lots of time preparing for the exam. Don't let an empty stomach get in the way of success!

When travelling to the testing center, leave earlier than needed. That way, you have a buffer in case you experience any delays. This will help you remain calm and will keep you from missing your appointment time at the testing center.

Be sure to pace yourself during the exam. Don't try to rush through the exam. There is no need to risk performing poorly on the exam just so you can leave the testing center early. Allow yourself to use all of the allotted time if needed.

Remain positive while taking the exam even if you feel like you are performing poorly. Thinking about the content you should have mastered will not help you perform better on the exam.

Once the exam is complete, take some time to relax. Even if you feel that you need to take the exam again, you will be well served by some down time before you begin studying again. It's often easier to convince yourself to study if you know that it will come with a reward!

Test-Taking Strategies

1. Predicting the Answer

When you feel confident in your preparation for a multiple-choice test, try predicting the answer before reading the answer choices. This is especially useful on questions that test objective factual knowledge. By predicting the answer before reading the available choices, you eliminate the possibility that you will be distracted or led astray by an incorrect answer choice. You will feel more confident in your selection if you read the question, predict the answer, and then find your prediction among the answer choices. After using this strategy, be sure to still read all of the answer choices carefully and completely. If you feel unprepared, you should not attempt to predict the answers. This would be a waste of time and an opportunity for your mind to wander in the wrong direction.

2. Reading the Whole Question

Too often, test takers scan a multiple-choice question, recognize a few familiar words, and immediately jump to the answer choices. Test authors are aware of this common impatience, and they will sometimes prey upon it. For instance, a test author might subtly turn the question into a negative, or he or she might redirect the focus of the question right at the end. The only way to avoid falling into these traps is to read the entirety of the question carefully before reading the answer choices.

3. Looking for Wrong Answers

Long and complicated multiple-choice questions can be intimidating. One way to simplify a difficult multiple-choice question is to eliminate all of the answer choices that are clearly wrong. In most sets of answers, there will be at least one selection that can be dismissed right away. If the test is administered on paper, the test taker could draw a line through it to indicate that it may be ignored; otherwise, the test taker will have to perform this operation mentally or on scratch paper. In either case, once the obviously incorrect answers have been eliminated, the remaining choices may be considered. Sometimes identifying the clearly wrong answers will give the test taker some information about the correct answer. For instance, if one of the remaining answer choices is a direct opposite of one of the eliminated answer choices, it may well be the correct answer. The opposite of obviously wrong is obviously right! Of course, this is not always the case. Some answers are obviously incorrect simply because they are irrelevant to the question being asked. Still, identifying and eliminating some incorrect answer choices is a good way to simplify a multiple-choice question.

4. Don't Overanalyze

Anxious test takers often overanalyze questions. When you are nervous, your brain will often run wild, causing you to make associations and discover clues that don't actually exist. If you feel that this may be a problem for you, do whatever you can to slow down during the test. Try taking a deep breath or counting to ten. As you read and consider the question, restrict yourself to the particular words used by the author. Avoid thought tangents about what the author *really* meant, or what he or she was *trying* to say. The only things that matter on a multiple-choice test are the words that are actually in the question. You must avoid reading too much into a multiple-choice question, or supposing that the writer meant something other than what he or she wrote.

5. No Need for Panic

It is wise to learn as many strategies as possible before taking a multiple-choice test, but it is likely that you will come across a few questions for which you simply don't know the answer. In this situation, avoid panicking. Because most multiple-choice tests include dozens of questions, the relative value of a single wrong answer is small. As much as possible, you should compartmentalize each question on a multiple-choice test. In other words, you should not allow your feelings about one question to affect your success on the others. When you find a question that you either don't understand or don't know how to answer, just take a deep breath and do your best. Read the entire question slowly and carefully. Try rephrasing the question a couple of different ways. Then, read all of the answer choices carefully. After eliminating obviously wrong answers, make a selection and move on to the next question.

6. Confusing Answer Choices

When working on a difficult multiple-choice question, there may be a tendency to focus on the answer choices that are the easiest to understand. Many people, whether consciously or not, gravitate to the answer choices that require the least concentration, knowledge, and memory. This is a mistake. When you come across an answer choice that is confusing, you should give it extra attention. A question might be confusing because you do not know the subject matter to which it refers. If this is the case, don't eliminate the answer before you have affirmatively settled on another. When you come across an answer choice of this type, set it aside as you look at the remaining choices. If you can confidently assert that one of the other choices is correct, you can leave the confusing answer aside. Otherwise, you will need to take a moment to try to better understand the confusing answer choice. Rephrasing is one way to tease out the sense of a confusing answer choice.

7. Your First Instinct

Many people struggle with multiple-choice tests because they overthink the questions. If you have studied sufficiently for the test, you should be prepared to trust your first instinct once you have carefully and completely read the question and all of the answer choices. There is a great deal of research suggesting that the mind can come to the correct conclusion very quickly once it has obtained all of the relevant information. At times, it may seem to you as if your intuition is working faster even than your reasoning mind. This may in fact be true. The knowledge you obtain while studying may be retrieved from your subconscious before you have a chance to work out the associations that support it. Verify your instinct by working out the reasons that it should be trusted.

8. Key Words

Many test takers struggle with multiple-choice questions because they have poor reading comprehension skills. Quickly reading and understanding a multiple-choice question requires a mixture of skill and experience. To help with this, try jotting down a few key words and phrases on a piece of scrap paper. Doing this concentrates the process of reading and forces the mind to weigh the relative importance of the question's parts. In selecting words and phrases to write down, the test taker thinks about the question more deeply and carefully. This is especially true for multiple-choice questions that are preceded by a long prompt.

9. Subtle Negatives

One of the oldest tricks in the multiple-choice test writer's book is to subtly reverse the meaning of a question with a word like *not* or *except*. If you are not paying attention to each word in the question, you can easily be led astray by this trick. For instance, a common question format is, "Which of the following is...?" Obviously, if the question instead is, "Which of the following is not...?," then the answer will be quite different. Even worse, the test makers are aware of the potential for this mistake and will include one answer choice that would be correct if the question were not negated or reversed. A test taker who misses the reversal will find what he or she believes to be a correct answer and will be so confident that he or she will fail to reread the question and discover the original error. The only way to avoid this is to practice a wide variety of multiple-choice questions and to pay close attention to each and every word.

10. Reading Every Answer Choice

It may seem obvious, but you should always read every one of the answer choices! Too many test takers fall into the habit of scanning the question and assuming that they understand the question because they recognize a few key words. From there, they pick the first answer choice that answers the question they believe they have read. Test takers who read all of the answer choices might discover that one of the latter answer choices is actually *more* correct. Moreover, reading all of the answer choices can remind you of facts related to the question that can help you arrive at the correct answer. Sometimes, a misstatement or incorrect detail in one of the latter answer choices will trigger your memory of the subject and will enable you to find the right answer. Failing to read all of the answer choices is like not reading all of the items on a restaurant menu: you might miss out on the perfect choice.

11. Spot the Hedges

One of the keys to success on multiple-choice tests is paying close attention to every word. This is never truer than with words like almost, most, some, and sometimes. These words are called "hedges" because they indicate that a statement is not totally true or not true in every place and time. An absolute statement will contain no hedges, but in many subjects, the answers are not always straightforward or absolute. There are always exceptions to the rules in these subjects. For this reason, you should favor those multiple-choice questions that contain hedging language. The presence of qualifying words indicates that the author is taking special care with his or her words, which is certainly important when composing the right answer. After all, there are many ways to be wrong, but there is only one way to be right! For this reason, it is wise to avoid answers that are absolute when taking a multiple-choice test. An absolute answer is one that says things are either all one way or all another. They often include words like *every*, *always*, *best*, and *never*. If you are taking a multiple-choice test in a subject that doesn't lend itself to absolute answers, be on your guard if you see any of these words.

12. Long Answers

In many subject areas, the answers are not simple. As already mentioned, the right answer often requires hedges. Another common feature of the answers to a complex or subjective question are qualifying clauses, which are groups of words that subtly modify the meaning of the sentence. If the question or answer choice describes a rule to which there are exceptions or the subject matter is complicated, ambiguous, or confusing, the correct answer will require many words in order to be expressed clearly and accurately. In essence, you should not be deterred by answer choices that seem excessively long. Oftentimes, the author of the text will not be able to write the correct answer without offering some qualifications and modifications. Your job is to read the answer choices thoroughly and completely and to select the one that most accurately and precisely answers the question.

13. Restating to Understand

Sometimes, a question on a multiple-choice test is difficult not because of what it asks but because of how it is written. If this is the case, restate the question or answer choice in different words. This process serves a couple of important purposes. First, it forces you to concentrate on the core of the question. In order to rephrase the question accurately, you have to understand it well. Rephrasing the question will concentrate your mind on the key words and ideas. Second, it will present the information to your mind in a fresh way. This process may trigger your memory and render some useful scrap of information picked up while studying.

14. True Statements

Sometimes an answer choice will be true in itself, but it does not answer the question. This is one of the main reasons why it is essential to read the question carefully and completely before proceeding to the answer choices. Too often, test takers skip ahead to the answer choices and look for true statements. Having found one of these, they are content to select it without reference to the question above. Obviously, this provides an easy way for test makers to play tricks. The savvy test taker will always read the entire question before turning to the answer choices. Then, having settled on a correct answer choice, he or she will refer to the original question and ensure that the selected answer is relevant. The mistake of choosing a correct-but-irrelevant answer choice is especially common on questions related to specific pieces of objective knowledge. A prepared test taker will have a wealth of factual knowledge at his or her disposal, and should not be careless in its application.

15. No Patterns

One of the more dangerous ideas that circulates about multiple-choice tests is that the correct answers tend to fall into patterns. These erroneous ideas range from a belief that B and C are the most common right answers, to the idea that an unprepared test-taker should answer "A-B-A-C-A-D-A-B-A." It cannot be emphasized enough that pattern-seeking of this type is exactly the WRONG way to approach a multiple-choice test. To begin with, it is highly unlikely that the test maker will plot the correct answers according to some predetermined pattern. The questions are scrambled and delivered in a random order. Furthermore, even if the test maker was following a pattern in the assignation of correct answers, there is no reason why the test taker would know which pattern he or she was using. Any attempt to discern a pattern in the answer choices is a waste of time and a distraction from the real work of taking the test. A test taker would be much better served by extra preparation before the test than by reliance on a pattern in the answers.

FREE DVD OFFER

Don't forget that doing well on your exam includes both understanding the test content and understanding how to use what you know to do well on the test. We offer a completely FREE Test Taking Tips DVD that covers world class test taking tips that you can use to be even more successful when you are taking your test.

All that we ask is that you email us your feedback about your study guide. To get your **FREE Test Taking Tips DVD**, email freedvd@studyguideteam.com with "FREE DVD" in the subject line and the following information in the body of the email:

- The title of your study guide.
- Your product rating on a scale of 1-5, with 5 being the highest rating.
- Your feedback about the study guide. What did you think of it?
- Your full name and shipping address to send your free DVD.

Introduction

Function of the Test

The Praxis Teaching Reading: Elementary Education Exam is for students or professionals entering or completing teacher preparation programs. It is required in 40 states for teacher licensure, and scores are transferrable for those wishing to move between states. This exam measures the ability of an individual to teach oral language and reading development at an elementary level. As identified by the National Reading Panel, it covers the five most important aspects of teaching reading instruction: phonemic awareness, phonics, fluency, vocabulary, and comprehension. This exam is offered nationwide through a variety of testing locations. The number of people who took the Praxis Teaching Reading Exam in the 2017–2018 year was 5,079.

Test Administration

The Praxis Teaching Reading Exam is offered five times during the 2019 year. The teaching window occurs for approximately a two-week span in January, March, April, May, and July. You can register to take the exam on the ETS Praxis website, and an available listing of test sites will be available for you to choose from. Retesting is available once every 21 days, or after 21 days for subject tests. Praxis tests are offered through the Educational Testing Service (ETS), and ETS is dedicated to providing accommodations to persons who have disabilities. Some accommodations should be requested, so visit the ETS website to find out more.

Test Format

The testing room prohibits cell phone use, and you are not allowed to bring in personal items, beverages, study materials, pencils, pens, calculators, or any electronic device of any kind. Personal items are not allowed in the test room, so if your facility does not provide storage, you must plan accordingly.

The Praxis Teaching Reading Exam is a 2.5-hour test with 90 selected-response questions and 3 constructed-response questions. The selected-response questions count for 75% of the total test score, and the constructed-response questions count for 25% of the total test score.

The table below shows a breakdown of the content domains:

Content Category	Number of Questions	Percentage of Exam
Assessment and Diagnostic Teaching of Reading	22 SR and 1 CR	27%
Reading Development • Phonemic Awareness and Oral Language Development • Phonics and Alphabetic Principle • Word-Analysis Skills and Vocabulary Development • Development of Reading Fluency and Reading Comprehension • Reading Comprehension Strategies Across Text Types	45 SR and 1 CR	46%
Writing in Support of Reading • Interdependence of Reading and Writing Development • Reading and Writing as Tools for Inquiry and Research	23 SR and 1 CR	27%

Scoring

The passing score for the Praxis Teaching Reading Exam depends on particular state requirements. You will be notified of a passing score after you take the exam and your states have been entered into the system. A list of states and passing scores are also available on the ETS website. The highest score of any other Praxis tests you have taken in the past ten years will show up on your score report along with your new score. End scores reveal how you did in each content, so if you choose to retake the exam, you will know which areas to focus on the most. All scores for Praxis exams are valid for ten years.

Recent/Future Developments

Praxis exams are updated on a regular basis to align with new core content. Test scores, however, will be valid for a ten-year period regardless of whether or not the content is still relevant.

Assessment and Diagnostic Teaching of Reading

Formal and Informal Reading Assessments

Formal and Informal Assessments

Formal assessments, such as selected-response questions, are a useful and quick way to grade students as opposed to free response assessments. However, informal assessments are an even quicker and more frequently used method of assessing students. Informal assessments can be conducted after a modeled lesson and before independent practice. The use of individual whiteboards and a few quick selected response questions prepared before the lesson is a helpful tactic for teachers to quickly survey which students grasped the concepts and which students need additional reinforcement. Those who still need to master the skill can then be efficiently identified and grouped together for a small reteach.

Demonstrating Ability to Interpret Results

When using the results from formal assessments addressing multiple skills, it is important to group students according to ability for the particular skill of interest from the assessment and not just on the overall score. However, the overall score may be beneficial for grouping with regards to pacing and complexity of questions.

Results of Assessments

Grouping students should be continuous and change daily, or at least weekly. Each student's needs change from concept to concept. Assessments must be ongoing and frequent. Results from these ongoing assessments should be the driving force behind the grouping of students. Lessons and groups should be adjusted to the needs of the students.

How Assessment Data are Used to Diagnose Reading Needs

Assessments are useful for identifying which students may be struggling with certain criteria as well as the specific areas of difficulty. Assessments can also indicate how well the material is being presented or provide vital clues on how to modify an individual student's instruction to help them grasp the content better. Generally, two types of assessments are used: informal and formal.

Informal assessments are not planned and lack a typical format or timeline. They can be as simple as watching and listening to how the students respond to answers in class or perform classwork. Observation is key. The instructor should be perceptive to how students not only respond to reading and language concepts but also to how they are interpreting them. If a student isn't understanding something such as a cultural reading concept, it may indicate that a more in-depth explanation is required. This will help the teacher adapt the instruction to enable the student to self-correct his or her own performance.

Formal assessments are partially based on observation, but are planned and implemented with the design to see how students respond to specific stimuli. They give a clearer indication of where students' weaknesses lie or whether they are on point in grasping the material. There are two primary methods for conducting formal assessments. The most conventional is a simple pencil-and-paper test in which students read prewritten questions and respond to them in writing. These physical answers provide a direct window into what the students know and how their reading comprehension is progressing. **Performance assessments** are a little less concrete but can provide a lot of insight into the student's mind-set and reactions that are more three-dimensional than a written assessment. This method does not use written responses, but instead analyzes students' performance in response to reading questions or activities. When giving performance assessments, it's important to bear in mind key questions: Does the student understand what they just read, did they seem uncomfortable when presenting their answer, and how accurate was their response? From here, new teaching strategies can be implemented, or the instructor can identify ways to provide specialized assistance to boost students' skills.

How Diagnostic Reading Data Addresses the Needs of Students with Reading Difficulties

Depending on where diagnostic data indicates areas of students' difficulty, reteaching certain material is a promising starting point to help students overcome their reading issues. This isn't a step backward in instruction; it's an alteration. Differentiated instruction offers opportunities for students to relearn reading principles in ways that best fit them individually.

If students are having reading difficulties, the lessons can be modified to be clearer or address the specific areas of difficulty. Sometimes, this means teaching the material in a different way entirely. Recalling the areas of differentiated instruction, there are many components of reading skills and understanding. If a student is having difficulty in one area, such as reading analysis, building on his or her conceptual knowledge and performance/evaluation reading skills could help connect the gaps in his or her analysis. For example, instead of just reading and responding to questions, students might grasp the material better through the use of simple logic. Breaking down sentence context and discussing the reading, rather than just asking questions and giving answers, can help bridge the gap in understanding, thus allowing students to draw further insight from the reading.

Considering what kind of activities improve which aspects of reading is also important. If students have phonetic problems, instructors should introduce activities that analyze the different aspects of words, as well as sounding out words, to build familiarity with English vocabulary and structure. To strengthen reading comprehension, incorporating activities that help students visualize what they read will help. Instructors should encourage students to paraphrase and summarize texts to examine their strengths and weaknesses as well. This will help the instructor identify what kind of differentiation may be necessary. Instead of shying away from challenging areas, it's important to modify lessons to help students approach the material with better focus and a renewed interest.

Student engagement will be instrumental in improving reading skills. Again, differential instruction encourages not only differentiated lessons and activities based on student ability, but also on interest. Having students design their own reading activities allows them to expand their skill sets while becoming eager to learn more. Activities such as synonym association for vocabulary words or even physically drawing out a given sentence will engage reading comprehension, analysis, and replication skills. Further assessments should be done to gauge the effectiveness of the new instruction methods.

How Diagnostic Reading Data are Used to Accelerate the Development of Reading Skills

Whether an instructor uses informal or formal assessment, **data** will be produced from the assessment. This data, both written or gained through observation, is highly valuable in diagnosing whether to change teaching methods in order to accelerate students' reading skills development. Data-driven instruction guides reading improvement for all students simply because the data provides clear indications of where students are facing reading challenges or demonstrating strengths.

Differentiated instruction acknowledges that, while a group of students may be learning the same subject, the way each student learns and processes the subject is different. This technique looks at the different learning methods and reading areas that students respond best to in order to effect change.

Therefore, an educator can then tailor, or differentiate, lessons to build on these skills and expedite the learning process. Differentiated instruction is divided into interest-based and ability-based instruction.

Much of a student's performance is based on their interest in the subject at hand. Sometimes a student may show difficulty reading because he or she isn't engaged in the material. One way to encourage reading growth is to allow students to choose their learning activities. This will give students ownership over their own education, enabling them to have fun while learning and to use specific activities they feel help them improve their reading abilities. For example, students more interested in visual activities may find reading more beneficial than listening to oral reading exercises.

Ability-based differentiation focuses on three core focus areas that determine reading proficiency and build skill. The first area of focus examines students' conceptual understanding of reading. If a teacher uses vocabulary or reading comprehension exercises in class, they will be able to examine how students are performing and modify instruction to address any confusion. This can also indicate students' preferences as well. The second differentiation looks at how students analyze and use the reading. Instructors must look at how students respond to questions and whether their interpretation is accurate. The final differentiation looks at how students evaluate and perform reading, creating a reaction that responds to the reading. The third differentiation looks at interpretation with the added step of using this knowledge to write or say something without being prompted that involves the reading. Identifying issues in one of these areas will narrow down where more emphasis must be placed to improve reading skills. Each reading area will affect the other two; improving one differentiated area will impact the others.

Flexible Grouping and Addressing Changing Reading Needs

Another way to differentiate instruction is the use of groups and collaboration in going over or learning the reading material. In class, there are two forms of grouping instruction: teacher-based and student-based. A well-balanced and flexible learning environment will incorporate both types of grouping exercises to help students approach reading from multiple angles and practice problem-solving and critical-thinking skills. Students also strengthen social skills through flexible grouping.

Teacher-based grouping is organized by the instructor. This is the best method for introducing students to new material and exploring key concepts. Instructors may also choose to break the class up into small groups to provide instruction and work with students individually while the class is working. The goal here is to monitor students directly and provide differentiated instruction when necessary. This is the more variable of the two groupings and provides a more direct line for teacher intervention. However, students can also grasp concepts by interacting with their peers.

Student-based grouping focuses on students dictating the way the group is formed, essentially freeing the teacher to observe how they are interacting with others and approaching reading topics. Students can be given the option to form their groups independently or simply opening the class to a group discussion. This is different from actually lecturing because it allows students to talk about the reading subject among themselves as opposed to just listening and learning from the instructor. Posing questions for the class is a great way for students to learn correct answers and ask questions through simple conversation. Student-based groups are also excellent for school projects, allowing group members to pool their knowledge for success.

Flexible grouping relies on utilizing both teacher-based and student-based groupings throughout the instructional period. Using one more than the other isn't necessarily unbalanced, but the instructor should try to incorporate both groupings in order to broaden the students' experience. The teacher's choice in using either method should also relate to how they are implementing differentiated teaching methods. Educators can combine the use of grouping to suit activities and lessons for all areas in which students may be facing difficulties in order to boost confidence and clarify material.

Response to Intervention (RTI) Process

Response to Intervention Process (RTI) is a process designed to help struggling students catch up through intervention and monitoring in a general education classroom. Students who suffer from undiagnosed reading disorders, attention issues, or even ESL students struggling to learn the language may begin to fall behind the rest of the students in reading skills. RTI is an informal intervention process done by the school that focuses on utilizing research and technology to help the student "catch up" to the rest of the class. The school's RTI teams will review assessments taken of each child in the classroom to determine which students need these instructional interventions. Teachers track students through **progress monitoring,** a process that measures whether or not the interventions are making a difference.

Although there are various ways to do RTI, it is usually set up as a three-tier system of support, also known as **multi-tier system of supports** (MTSS). The tiers below are in order of least intense to most intense:

Tier 1: High-Quality Classroom Instruction, Screening, and Group Interventions
In Tier 1 interventions, the entire classroom is assessed using **universal screening**, where everyone's skillset is measured in a general education classroom by using methods that have been proven to be effective. Students who receive Tier 1 support are generally divided into small groups based on their skill level. Many students receive Tier 1 support because their math or reading skills are not quite at grade level. Progress of Tier 1 instruction is monitored, and many students are able to effectively catch up to grade level.

Tier 2: Targeted Interventions
Tier 2 interventions are for students who do not yet reach the potential of Tier 1 intervention. **Targeted interventions** give more detailed attention to the student who is struggling in addition to the regular classroom instruction. Since targeted interventions are done in addition to the regular classroom instruction, they are sometimes conducted during extracurricular activities or electives.

Tier 3: Intensive Interventions and Comprehensive Evaluation
The third tier of the RTI process is **intensive intervention**. Intensive interventions are often done one-on-one or in small groups with other special-needs children. Usually only one or two students in a classroom will need this kind of instruction, so one-on-one help is more readily available for this tier.

Practice Questions

1. In the word *shut*, the *sh* is an example of what?
    a. Consonant digraph
    b. Sound segmentation
    c. Vowel digraph
    d. Rime

2. When students identify the phonemes in spoken words, they are practicing which of the following?
    a. Sound blending
    b. Substitution
    c. Rhyming
    d. Segmentation

3. What is the alphabetic principle?
    a. The understanding that letters represent sounds in words.
    b. The ability to combine letters to correctly spell words.
    c. The proper use of punctuation within writing.
    d. The memorization of all the letters in the alphabet.

4. Print awareness includes all EXCEPT which of the following concepts?
    a. The differentiation of uppercase and lowercase letters
    b. The identification of word boundaries
    c. The proper tracking of words
    d. The spelling of sight words

5. When teachers point to words during shared readings, what are they modeling?
    I. Word boundaries
    II. Directionality
    III. One-to-one correspondence
    a. I and II
    b. I and III
    c. II and III
    d. I, II, and III

6. Structural analysis would be the most appropriate strategy in determining the meaning of which of the following words?
    a. Extra
    b. Improbable
    c. Likely
    d. Wonder

7. A student spells *eagle* as *EGL.* This student is performing at which stage of spelling?
    a. Conventional
    b. Phonetic
    c. Semiphonetic
    d. Transitional

8. Spelling instruction should include which of the following?

      I. Word walls

      II. Daily reading opportunities

      III. Daily writing opportunities

      IV. Weekly spelling inventories with words students have studied during the week

    a. I and IV

    b. I, II, and III

    c. I, II, and IV

    d. I, II, III, and IV

9. A kindergarten student is having difficulty distinguishing the letters *b* and *d*. The teacher should do which of the following?

    a. Have the student use a think-aloud to verbalize the directions of the shapes used when writing each letter.

    b. Have the student identify the letters within grade-appropriate texts.

    c. Have the student write each letter five times.

    d. Have the student write a sentence in which all of the letters start with either *b* or *d*.

10. When differentiating phonics instruction for English-language learners (ELLs), teachers should do which of the following?

    a. Increase the rate of instruction

    b. Begin with the identification of word boundaries

    c. Focus on syllabication

    d. Capitalize on the transfer of relevant skills from the learners' original language(s)

11. Which of the following is the most appropriate assessment of spelling for students who are performing at the pre-phonetic stage?

    a. Sight word drills

    b. Phonemic awareness tests

    c. Writing samples

    d. Concepts about print (CAP) test

12. Phonological awareness is best assessed through which of the following?

    a. Identification of rimes or onsets within words

    b. Identification of letter-sound correspondences

    c. Comprehension of an audio book

    d. Writing samples

13. The identification of morphemes within words occurs during the instruction of what?

    a. Structural analysis

    b. Syllabic analysis

    c. Phonics

    d. The alphabetic principle

14. Which of the following pairs of words are homophones?

    a. Playful and replay

    b. To and too

    c. Was and were

    d. Gloomy and sad

15. Nursery rhymes are used in kindergarten to develop what?
    a. Print awareness
    b. Phoneme recognition
    c. Syllabication
    d. Structural analysis

16. High-frequency words such as *be, the*, and *or* are taught during the instruction of what?
    a. Phonics skills
    b. Sight word recognition
    c. Vocabulary development
    d. Structural analysis

17. To thoroughly assess students' phonics skills, teachers should administer assessments that require students to do which of the following?
    a. Decode in context only
    b. Decode in isolation only
    c. Both A and B
    d. Neither A nor B

18. A student is having difficulty pronouncing a word that she comes across when reading aloud. Which of the following is most likely NOT a reason for the difficulty that the student is experiencing?
    a. Poor word recognition
    b. A lack of content vocabulary
    c. Inadequate background knowledge
    d. Repeated readings

19. Which is the largest contributor to the development of students' written vocabulary?
    a. Reading
    b. Directed reading
    c. Direct teaching
    d. Modeling

20. The study of roots, suffixes, and prefixes is called what?
    a. Listening comprehension
    b. Word consciousness
    c. Word morphology
    d. Textual analysis

21. When children begin to negotiate the sounds that make up words in their language independently, what skill/s are they demonstrating?
    a. Phonological awareness
    b. Phonemes
    c. Phoneme substitution
    d. Blending skills

22. What is phonics?
    a. The study of syllabication
    b. The study of onsets and rimes
    c. The study of sound-letter relationships
    d. The study of graphemes

23. Word analysis skills are NOT critical for the development of what area of literacy?
    a. Vocabulary
    b. Reading fluency
    c. Spelling
    d. Articulation

24. What area of study involves mechanics, usage, and sentence formation?
    a. Word analysis
    b. Spelling conventions
    c. Morphemes
    d. Phonics

Answer Explanations

1. A: The *sh* is an example of a consonant digraph. Consonant diagraphs are combinations of two or three combinations of consonants that work together to make a single sound. Examples of consonant digraphs are *sh*, *ch*, and *th*. Choice B, sound segmentation, is used to identify component phonemes in a word, such as separating the /t/, /u/, and /b/ for *tub*. Choice C, vowel digraph, are sets of two vowels that make up a single sound, such as *ow*, *ae*, or *ie*. Choice D, rime, is the sound that follows a word's onset, such as the /at/ in *cat*.

2. D: Sound segmentation is the identification of all the component phonemes in a word. An example would be the student identifying each separate sound, /t/, /u/, and /b/, in the word *tub*. Choice A, sound blending, is the blending together of two or more sounds in a word, such as /ch/ or /sh/. Choice B, substitution, occurs when a phoneme is substituted within a word for another phoneme, such as substituting the sound /b/ in *bun* to /r/ to create *run*. Choice C, rhyming, is an effective tool to utilize during the analytic phase of phonics development because rhyming words are often identical except for their beginning letters.

3. A: The alphabetical principle is the understanding that letters represent sounds in words. It is through the alphabetic principle that students learn the interrelationships between letter-sound (grapheme-phoneme) correspondences, phonemic awareness, and early decoding skills (such as sounding out and blending letter sounds).

4. D: Print awareness includes all except the spelling of sight words. Print awareness includes Choice A, the differentiation of uppercase and lowercase letters, so that students can understand which words begin a sentence. Choice B, the identification of word boundaries, is also included in print awareness; that is, students should be made aware that words are made up of letters and that spaces appear between words, etc. Choice C, the proper tracking of words, is also included in print awareness; this is the realization that print is organized in a particular way, so books must be tracked and held accordingly.

5. D: Word boundaries is included as one of the factors modeled because students should be able to identify which letters make up a word as well as the spaces before and after the letters that make up words. Directionality is the ability to track words as they are being read, so this is also modeled. One-to-one correspondence, the last factor listed, is the ability to match written letters to words to a spoken word when reading. It is another thing teachers model when they point to words while they read.

6. B: Structural analysis focuses on the meaning of morphemes. Morphemes include base words, prefixes, and word endings (inflections and suffixes) that are found within longer words. Students can use structural analysis skill to find familiar word parts within an unfamiliar word in order to decode the word and determine the definition of the new word. The prefix im- (meaning not) in the word "improbable" can help students derive the definition of an event that is not likely to occur.

7. B: The student is performing at the phonetic stage. Phonetic spellers will spell a word as it sounds. The speller perceives and represents all of the phonemes in a word. However, because phonetic spellers have limited sight word vocabulary, irregular words are often spelled incorrectly.

8. B: The creation of word walls, Choice *I*, is advantageous during the phonetic stage of spelling development. On a word wall, words that share common consonant-vowel patterns or letter clusters are written in groups. Choices *II* and *III*, daily reading and writing opportunities, are also important in spelling instructions. Students need daily opportunities in order to review and practice spelling development. Daily journals or exit tickets are cognitive writing strategies effective in helping students reflect on what they have learned. A spelling inventory, Choice *IV,* is different than a traditional spelling test because students are not allowed to study the words prior to the administration of a spelling inventory. Therefore, this option is incorrect as it mentions the inventory contains words students have studied all week.

9. A: The teacher should have the student use a think-aloud to verbalize the directions of the shapes used when writing each letter. During think-alouds, teachers voice the metacognitive process that occurs when writing each part of a given letter. Students should be encouraged to do likewise when practicing writing the letters.

10. D: Teachers should capitalize on the transfer of relevant skills from the learner's original language(s). In this way, extra attention and instructional emphasis can be applied toward the teaching of sounds and meanings of words that are nontransferable between the two languages.

11. C: Writing sample are the most appropriate assessment of spelling for students who are performing at the pre-phonetic stage s. During the pre-phonetic stage, students participate in precommunicative writing. Precommunicative writing appears to be a jumble of letter-like forms rather than a series of discrete letters. Samples of students' precommunicative writing can be used to assess their understanding of the alphabetic principle and their knowledge of letter-sound correspondences.

12. A: Phonological awareness is best assessed through identification of rimes or onsets within words. Instruction of phonological awareness includes detecting and identifying word boundaries, syllables, onset/rime, and rhyming words.

13. A: The identification of morphemes within words occurs during the instruction of structural analysis. Structural analysis is a word recognition skill that focuses on the meaning of word parts, or morphemes, during the introduction of a new word. Choice *B,* syllabic analysis, is a word analysis skill that helps students split words into syllables. Choice *C,* phonics, is the direct correspondence between and blending of letters and sounds. Choice *D,* the alphabetic principle, teaches that letters or other characters represent sounds.

14. B: Homophones are words that are pronounced the same way but differ in meaning and/or spelling. The pair *to* and *too* is an example of a homophone because they are pronounced the same way, but differ in both meaning and spelling. Choices *A, C,* and *D* are not homophones because they do not sound the same when spoken aloud.

15. B: Nursery rhymes are used in kindergarten to develop phoneme recognition. Rhyming words are often almost identical except for their beginning letter(s), so rhyming is a great strategy to implement during the analytic phase of phoneme development.

16. B: High-frequency words are taught during the instruction of sight word recognition. Sight words, sometimes referred to as high-frequency words, are words that are used often but may not follow the regular principles of phonics. Sight words may also be defined as words that students are able to recognize and read without having to sound out.

17. C: Both *A* and *B*. Decoding should be assessed in context in addition to isolation. During such assessments, the students read passages from reading-level appropriate texts aloud to the teacher so that the teacher is better able to analyze a student's approach to figuring out unknown words. Decoding should also be assessed in isolation. In these types of assessments, students are given a list of words and/or phonics patterns. Initially, high-frequency words that follow predictable phonics patterns are presented. The words that are presented become more challenging as a student masters less difficult words.

18. D: An individual's sight vocabulary includes the words that he or she can recognize and correctly pronounce when reading. Limited sight vocabulary can be caused by poor word recognition, a lack of content vocabulary, and inadequate background knowledge. Although proper pronunciation may affect the ability to spell a word, the ability to properly spell a word is less likely to affect a student's ability to properly pronounce that word.

19. A: There is a positive correlation between a student's exposure to text and the academic achievement of that individual. Therefore, students should be given ample opportunities to read independently as much text as possible in order to gain vocabulary and background knowledge.

20. C: By definition, morphology is the identification and use of morphemes such as root words and affixes. Listening comprehension refers to the processes involved in understanding spoken language. Word consciousness refers to the knowledge required for students to learn and effectively utilize language. Textual analysis is an approach that researchers use to gain information and describe the characteristics of a recorded or visual message.

21. A: Phonological Awareness refers to a child's ability to understand and use familiar sounds in his or her social environment in order to form coherent words. Phonemes are defined as distinct sound units in any given language. Phonemic substitution is part of phonological awareness—a child's ability to substitute specific phonemes for others. Blending skills refers to the ability to construct or build words from individual phonemes by blending the sounds together in a unique sequence.

22. C: When children begin to recognize and apply sound-letter relationships independently and accurately, they are demonstrating a growing mastery of phonics. Phonics is the most commonly used method for teaching people to read and write by associating sounds with their corresponding letters or groups of letters, using a language's alphabetic writing system. Syllabication refers to the ability to break down words into their individual syllables. The study of onsets and rimes strives to help students recognize and separate a word's beginning consonant or consonant-cluster sound—the onset—from the word's rime—the vowel and/or consonants that follow the onset. A grapheme is a letter or a group of letters in a language that represent a sound.

23. D: Breaking down words into their individual parts, studying prefixes, suffixes, root words, rimes, and onsets, are all examples of word analysis. When children analyze words, they develop their vocabulary and strengthen their spelling and reading fluency.

24. B: Spelling conventions is the area of study that involves mechanics, usage, and sentence formation. Mechanics refers to spelling, punctuation, and capitalization. Usage refers to the use of the various parts of speech within sentences, and sentence formation is the order in which the various words in a sentence appear. Generally speaking, word analysis is the breaking down of words into morphemes and word units in order to arrive at the word's meaning. Morphemes are the smallest units of a written language that carry meaning, and phonics refers to the study of letter-sound relationships.

Reading Development

Phonemic Awareness and Oral Language Development

Listening and speaking skills Communication is never one-sided. There are always at least two individuals engaged in a conversation, and both acts of speaking and listening are often interchangeable. In the classroom, educators communicate with all students, and students communicate with one another. Some forms of communication are intended for instructional purposes, while other forms may be solely for entertainment. To be an effective communicator, it is critical that the purpose for speaking is clear to both the presenter and the audience. It is also important that the mode of communication is culturally sensitive and age appropriate. The presenter should use language that best suits his or her audience. For example, if an educator wishes to speak to a primary class about the importance of homework, domain-specific language may not be appropriate, but that same conversation with educational colleagues may require domain-specific language. Here are some key techniques to consider when developing strong communication skills:

Effective Speaking	Effective Listening
Check for understanding and interest—ask key questions	Offer relevant information to the topic
Repeat important information in a variety of ways	Ask poignant questions, clarify understanding
Use nonverbal forms of communication—body language for effect	Use nonverbal forms of communication—body language for effect
Remain observant—maintain eye contact	Remain observant—maintain eye contact
Develop a healthy sense of humor	Develop a healthy sense of humor
Strive for honesty	Strive for honesty
Consider language choices	Develop active listening skills—not simply waiting to respond
Develop cultural sensitivity	Strengthen patience

Listening and Speaking Vocabularies

Vocabulary used throughout informational texts is generally quite different than vocabulary found in fictional print. For this reason, it is imperative that educators help children strengthen and increase their vocabulary inventory so that they can eventually become successful at reading and understanding informational text.

For instance, educators can point out *signal words* throughout texts to help children more readily and accurately identify the author's purpose. There are specific vocabulary words that authors employ that spotlight the author's intent. For instance, if authors wish to list examples to support a main idea, they may use vocabulary such as *for example*, *such as*, or *as illustrated*. When displaying the chronological order of events, authors may use *first*, *lastly*, *before*, and *finally*. Some common compare and contrast vocabulary words include *but*, *same as*, *similar to*, *as opposed to*, and *however*. There are several key phrases that signal cause and effect relationships, including *because of*, *as a result of*, and *in order to*.

Using word walls and personal dictionaries, sorting vocabulary words according to theme, introducing text maps, and teaching children to become familiar with sidebars and glossaries in informational texts, educators will help expand their students' vocabulary and strengthen their ability to read and comprehend informational texts successfully.

Methods for Scaffolding the Learning of Standard American English

English Language Learners (ELLs) or students with varying dialects may need alternate methods of instruction when it comes to the learning of standard American English. Scaffolding refers to techniques used that allow students to progress toward a greater level of understanding on an increasingly independent level. The teacher will help the student by gradually removing aid until the student can perform the task on their own. Although there are many different scaffolding techniques, a few common ones are presented below:

Connecting New Information to Prior Learning
When using the process of scaffolding, it's important that the EL student be guided through the activities from the start. Teachers will determine what level of aid to give to the student depending on their language level. One important method of scaffolding is using previous experience to connect to new information. Teachers should be knowledgeable of students' culture and world experiences in order to synthesize new and old information. Cultural relevance in the EL framework is crucial for the student to understand the importance of what's being taught.

Pre-Teach Academic Vocabulary Outright
Another method of scaffolding is the practice of teaching vocabulary before full immersion is taken place in the English language. Again, a collaborative effort will be most effective for this sort of learning experience. Having students work together to understand the vocabulary word, its meaning, as well as its idiomatic expressions along with frequent visits from the teacher might be a chance to learn vocabulary while also engaging in proximal social interactions. Word walls are also suggested at all levels to help students pronounce unfamiliar words as well as having visual contact with the word along with the auditory experience.

Make Lessons Visual by Using Graphic Organizers
Many students are visual learners, and even if they are not, visual learning is an appropriate aid to many other kinds of learners. This method of scaffolding is also beneficial in helping students develop creativity and work with others to collaboratively assist in each other's creativity and ideas. Graphic organizers include webs, Venn diagrams, story boards, KWL charts, spider maps, and charts, all of which help students organize information and develop higher-level thinking.

Engage English Learners in Discourse
Practicing language "out loud" creates a stimulating environment wherein the student can collaboratively work with others to immerse themselves in social and academic discourse. It's important to make sure academic language is included in this activity, as it is harder to learn and takes a structured environment facilitated by the instructor. Engagement in academic conversations can come before or during social conversations as well. Social conversation may come easier, but academic conversation is important to the classroom as well to aid in development toward future research, writing, and career development.

Age-Appropriate Milestones for Language Development

Developing Language Literacy Skills

It is believed that literacy development is the most rapid between birth and 5 years of age. From birth until around 3 months, babies start to recognize the sounds of familiar voices. Between 3 months and 6 months, babies begin to study a speaker's mouth and listen much more closely to speech sounds. Between 9 months and 12 months, babies can generally recognize a growing number of commonly repeated words, can utter simple words, respond appropriately to simple requests, and begin to attempt to group sounds.

In the toddler years, children begin to rapidly strengthen their communication skills, connecting sounds to meanings and combining sounds to create coherent sentences. The opportunities for rich social interactions play a key role in this early literacy development and help children to understand cultural nuances, expected behavior, and effective communication skills. By age 3, most toddlers can understand many sentences and can begin to generalize by placing specific words into categories. In the preschool years, children begin to develop and strengthen their emergent literacy skills. It is at this stage that children will begin to sound out words, learn basic spelling patterns, especially with rhyming words, and start to develop their fine motor skills. Awareness of basic grammar also begins to emerge with oral attempts at past, present, and future verb tenses.

English Literacy Development

English language literacy can be categorized into four basic stages:

- Beginning
- Early Intermediate
- Intermediate
- Early Advanced

Beginning Literacy

This stage is commonly referred to as **receptive language development**. Educators can encourage this stage in literacy development by providing the student with many opportunities to interact on a social level with peers. Educators should also consider starting a personal dictionary, introducing word flashcards, and providing the student with opportunities to listen to a story read by another peer, or as a computer-based activity.

Early Intermediate Literacy

When a child begins to communicate to express a need or attempt to ask or respond to a question, the child is said to be at the early intermediate literacy stage. Educators should continue to build vocabulary knowledge and introduce activities that require the student to complete the endings of sentences, fill in the blanks, and describe the beginning or ending of familiar stories.

Intermediate Literacy

When a child begins to demonstrate comprehension of more complex vocabulary and abstract ideas, the child is advancing into the intermediate literacy stage. It is at this stage that children are able to challenge themselves to meet the classroom learning expectations and start to use their newly acquired literacy skills to read, write, listen, and speak. Educators may consider providing students with more advanced reading opportunities, such as partner-shared reading, silent reading, and choral reading.

Early Advanced Literacy

When a child is able to apply literacy skills to learn new information across many subjects, the child is progressing toward the early advanced literacy stage. The child can now tackle complex literacy tasks and confidently handle much more cognitively demanding material. To strengthen reading comprehension, educators should consider the introduction to word webs and semantic organizers. Book reports and class presentations, as well as continued opportunities to access a variety of reading material, will help to strengthen the child's newly acquired literacy skills.

Linguistic and Cultural Diversity in a Learning Environment

The classroom must be a place that emphasizes respect for all individuals as well as collaboration to achieve a successful learning environment. In addition to teaching reading skills, the instructor is expected to be a model of tolerance and inclusiveness for all students, thus encouraging them to be open-minded toward others. In the United States, it's likely that instructors will have students from a broad range of cultural and linguistic backgrounds. Obviously, these students must be made to feel welcome, and any linguistic difficulties they have should be treated as simply another step in the learning process, not a result of their background. Any difficulty is an opportunity for the whole class to learn and grow.

Encouraging polite and respectful behavior is key. An instructor doesn't necessarily need to explain polite behavior, but rather, should serve as a role model for the class. When addressing students' issues, the teacher should be sensitive to how they feel and be encouraging no matter their religious or ethnic background. It's also important to monitor how students act and respond to one another. Proper language and behavior should be enforced when necessary, and if there is ever anything rude or insensitive said or done, it must be addressed and corrected. Teachers should emphasize the idea that, while everyone is different, they are all equal. Therefore, students must be treated respectfully. Teachers should observe whether students are listening to other students and not being distracted or showing signs of disrespect. Tone and physical behavior must also be monitored; there's no excuse for rudeness. When disrespect occurs, steps should be taken to ensure it isn't repeated. It's important to remember that behaviors and lessons in early learners will inform how children grow and mature.

Reading and writing activities can also provide lessons in respect and collaboration. For instance, students can do group work on a text that discusses respectful behavior for reading practice, and also talk about the meaning of the written content. Other lessons can look at readings from different cultures to expand the students' appreciation and interest in diversity.

Phonemic Awareness in Reading Development

A phoneme is the smallest unit of sound in a given language and is one aspect under the umbrella of skills associated with phonological awareness. A child demonstrates phonemic awareness when identifying rhymes, recognizing alliterations, and isolating specific sounds inside a word or a set of words. Students who demonstrate basic phonemic awareness will eventually also be able to independently and appropriately blend together a variety of phonemes.

Some classroom strategies to strengthen phonemic awareness may include:

- Introduction to nursery rhymes and word play
- Speech discrimination techniques to train the ear to hear more accurately
- Repeated instruction connecting sounds to letters and blending sounds
- Use of visual images coupled with corresponding sounds and words

- Teaching speech sounds through direct instruction
- Comparing known to unfamiliar words
- Practicing pronunciation of newly introduced letters, letter combinations, and words
- Practicing word decoding
- Differentiating similar sounding words

Development of Phonemic-Awareness Skills

Age-appropriate and developmentally appropriate instruction for phonological and phonemic awareness is key to helping children strengthen their reading and writing skills. Phonological and phonemic awareness, or PPA, instruction works to enhance correct speech, improve understanding and application of accurate letter-to-sound correspondence, and strengthen spelling skills. Since skill-building involving phonemes is not a natural process but needs to be taught, PPA instruction is especially important for children who have limited access and exposure to reading materials and who lack familial encouragement to read. Strategies that educators can implement include leading word and sound games, focusing on phoneme skill-building activities, and ensuring all activities focus on the fun, playful nature of words and sounds instead of rote memorization and drilling techniques.

Phonics and Alphabetic Principle

Automatic Word Recognition of High-Frequency Sight Words

Beginning readers enter primary school years with many challenges involving literacy development. Tackling the alphabetic principle and phonemic awareness helps children to recognize that specific sounds are usually comprised of specific letters, or a combination thereof, and that each letter or combination of letters carries a specific sound. However, these young readers are also faced with the challenge of sight word mastery. **Sight words** do not necessarily follow the alphabetic principle and appear quite often in primary reading material. Some sight words are decodable, but many are not, which requires the additional challenge of memorizing correct spelling. Some of these non-decodable sight words include words such as *who, the, he, does,* and so on. There are approximately one hundred sight words that appear throughout primary texts.

The goal for primary teachers is to help emergent readers to recognize these sight words automatically, in order to help strengthen reading fluency. One effective instructional approach is to provide children daily opportunities to practice sight words in meaningful contexts and to establish a clearly visible, large print word wall that children can freely access throughout the day. Dr. Edward William Dolch was a well-known and respected children's author and professor who, in the late 1940s, published a list of sight words he believed appeared most frequently in children's literature for grades kindergarten through second grade. Now known as the Dolch Word List, these sight words are still widely used in primary classrooms throughout the United States. Organized by grade and frequency, the Dolch Word List consists of 220 words in total, with the first one hundred known as the "Dolch 100 List." Dr. Edward Fry, a university professor, author, and expert in the field of reading, published another commonly used high-frequency word list approximately a decade later. Although similar in many ways to the Dolch List, the Fry Word List primarily focuses on sight words that appear most frequently in reading material for third to ninth grade. Other high-frequency word lists now exist, but the Dolch and Fry word lists are still widely used in today's elementary classrooms. The debate, however, is whether to teach high-frequency sight words in isolation or as part of the integrated phonics program.

Unlike many sight words, **decodable words** follow the rules of phonics and are spelled phonetically. They are spelled precisely the way they sound—as in words like *dad* and *sit*. When a child has mastered his or her phonics skills, these decodable words can also be easily mastered with continued opportunities to practice reading. Activities involving segmenting and blending decodable words also help to strengthen a child's decoding skills. Some educators will find that it is beneficial to integrate lessons involving decodable words and high-frequency sight words, while others may see a need to keep these lessons separate until children have demonstrated mastery or near mastery of phonemic awareness. Some activities that encourage the memorization of sight words and strengthen decoding skills involve the use of flash cards, phonemic awareness games, air writing, and card games, such as *Bingo* and *Go Fish*.

Both Dolch and Fry word lists are organized according to frequency and grade level. It is widely accepted that educators follow a cumulative approach to reading instruction, introducing high-frequency sight words that are also phonetically decodable. Should words appear in the lesson that are not phonetically decodable, educators may wish to use this as an opportunity to evaluate the children's phonemic awareness skills and determine whether or not students are ready for lessons that integrate non-decodable sight words. For instance, an educator might challenge a student to study the parts of the non-decodable sight word by asking whether or not there are parts of the word that are phonetically decodable and parts that are not. This approach gives students the opportunity for guided word study and acts as a bridge between phonemic awareness skills and sight word memorization.

Determining what lists of words to introduce to students varies greatly and depends on an initial and ongoing spelling assessment of each child to determine his or her current spelling and reading levels. Effective instructional approaches also involve the intentional selection of words that demonstrate a specific spelling pattern, followed by multiple opportunities to read, spell, segment, and blend these word families. Students will benefit the greatest with ongoing formative and summative assessments of their decoding skills as well as their ability to apply their word knowledge to and memorize non-decodable sight words.

With the reinforcement of high-frequency word walls, daily opportunities to read, write, and engage in meaningful word games and activities, children will gradually begin to develop their reading and spelling skills and learn to become more fluent and capable readers.

When students are invited to become word detectives, the study of root words and affixes is of prime importance. There are several instructional approaches to the study of root words and affixes, including a multi-sensory guided approach in which children can physically pull apart the affixes to be left with the root word and then manipulate the root word by playing with a variety of suffixes and prefixes. The following table begins with the original word containing both a prefix and suffix. The word is pulled apart into its individual components—root, prefix, and suffix. Then, it is given a new prefix and suffix to form a new word, carrying a completely new meaning:

Original Word	Root Word	Prefix	Suffix	New Prefix	New Suffix	New Word
inactive	act	in	ive	De	ate	deactivate
disbelieving	believe	dis	ing	Un	able	unbelievable
unbearable	bear	un	able	For	ing	forbearing

Effective instruction for root, prefix, and suffix study should involve the active exploration of words, with ample opportunity for children to read the words in meaningful context. Typically, a formal study of root words and affixes is introduced by the 4th grade, but it may be introduced earlier, depending on the students' understanding of basic phonics and spelling patterns. It is important for educators to keep in mind that new vocabulary terms, verb forms, plurals, and compound words may present a challenge for some students.

A formal study of root words, prefixes, and suffixes strengthens a child's knowledge of word meanings, expands vocabulary knowledge, and advances his or her understanding and application of various spelling patterns. Children will learn more about how affixes affect the spelling of the root word and can completely alter its meaning, which ultimately strengthens their ability to read, write, and spell accurately and effectively. As children become familiar with various affixes, they will begin to decipher the meaning of unfamiliar words that share the same affixes and roots.

Concepts of Print

Print awareness aids reading development, as it is the understanding that the printed word represents the ideas voiced in spoken language. Print awareness includes the understanding that:

>   1. Words are made of letters; spaces appear between words and words make sentences.

>   2. Print is organized in a particular way (e.g., read from left to right and top to bottom, read from front to back, etc.), so books must be tracked and held accordingly.

>   3. There are different types of print for different purposes (magazines, billboards, essays, fiction, etc.).

Print awareness provides the foundation on which all other literacy skills are built. It is often the first stage of reading development. Without print awareness, a student is not likely to develop letter-sound correspondence, word reading skills, or reading comprehension skills. For this reason, a child's performance on tasks relevant to their print awareness is indicative of the child's future reading achievement.

The following strategies can be used to increase print awareness in students:

>   1. *An adult reads aloud to students and shared reading experiences.* In order to maximize print awareness within the student, the reader should point out the form, function, orientation, and sounds of letters and words.

>   2. *Shared readings also build one-to-one correspondence.* **One-to-one correspondence** is the ability to match written letters or words to a spoken word when reading. This can be accomplished by pointing to words as they are read. This helps students make text-to-word connections. Pointing also aids **directionality**, or the ability to track the words that are being read.

>   3. *Use the child's environment.* To reinforce print awareness, teachers can make a child aware of print in their environment, such as words on traffic signs. Teachers can reinforce this by labeling objects in the classroom.

4. *Instruction of book organization can occur during read-alouds.* Students should be taught the proper orientation, tracking, and numbering conventions of books. For example, teachers can differentiate the title from the author's name on the front cover of a book.

5. *Let students practice.* Allowing students to practice book-handling skills with wordless, predictable, or patterned text will help to instill print awareness.

Recognizing Uppercase and Lowercase Letters

Among the skills that are used to determine reading readiness, letter identification is the strongest predictor. **Letter recognition** is the identification of each letter in the alphabet. Letter recognition does not include letter-sound correspondences; however, learning about and being able to recognize letters may increase student motivation to learn letter sounds. Also, the names of many letters are similar to their sounds, so letter recognition serves as a gateway for the letter-sound relationships that are needed for reading to occur. Similarly, the ability to differentiate between uppercase and lowercase letters is beneficial in determining where a sentence begins and ends.

To be fluent in letter identification, students should be able to identify letter names in and out of context with automaticity. In order to obtain such familiarity with the identification of letters, students need ample experience, acquaintance, and practice with letters. Explicit instruction in letter recognition, practice printing uppercase and lowercase letters of the alphabet, and consistent exposure to printed letters are essential in the instruction of letter recognition.

Research has revealed that the following sequencing guidelines are necessary to effectively promote letter naming and identification:

1. The initial stage includes visual discrimination of shapes and curved lines.

2. Once students are able to identify and discriminate shapes with ease, then letter formations can be introduced. During the introduction of letter shapes, two letters that share visual (*p* and *q*) or auditory (/a/ and /u/) similarities should never be presented in back-to-back.

3. Next, uppercase letters are introduced. Uppercase letters are introduced before lowercase letters because they are easier to discriminate visually than lowercase letters. When letter formations are first presented to a student, their visual system analyzes the vertical, horizontal, and curved orientations of the letters. Therefore, teachers should use think-alouds when instructing how to write the shape of each letter. During think-alouds, teachers verbalize their own thought processes that occur when writing each part of a given letter. Students should be encouraged to do likewise when practicing printing the letters.

4. Once uppercase letters are mastered, lowercase letters can be introduced. High-frequency lowercase letters (*a, e, t*) are introduced prior to low-frequency lowercase letters (*q, x, z*).

5. Once the recognition of letters is mastered, students need ample time manipulating and utilizing the letters. This can be done through sorting, matching, comparing, and writing activities.

Invented Spellings and Understanding of Phonetic Principles

When children begin to learn the various letter-sound correspondences, their phonemic awareness begins to overlap with their awareness of orthography and reading. One of the widely accepted strategies to employ when introducing children to letter-sound correspondences is to begin with those correspondences that occur the most frequently in simple English words. In an effort to help build confidence in young learners, educators are encouraged to introduce only a few letter-sound combinations at a time and provide ample opportunities for practice and review before introducing new combinations. Although there is no formally established order for the introduction of letter-sound correspondences, educators are encouraged to consider the following general guidelines, but they should also keep in mind the needs, experiences, and current literacy levels of the students. The following is intended as a general guide only:

1. a	6. n	11. g	16. l	21. x
2. m	7. c	12. h	17. e	22. v
3. t	8. d	13. i	18. r	23. y
4. p	9. u	14. f	19. w	24. z
5. o	10. s	15. b	20. k	25. j
				26. q

As a generally accepted rule, short vowels should be introduced ahead of long vowels, and lowercase letters should be mastered before the introduction of their upper case counterparts.

Spelling conventions in the English language are primarily concerned with three areas: mechanics, usage, and sentence formation.

Mechanics
For primary students who are just beginning to master the alphabetic principle, educators should first concentrate on proper letter formation, the spelling of high-frequency words and sight words, and offer classroom discussions to promote the sharing of ideas. When children begin to write in sentences to share their thoughts and feelings in print, educators may consider the introduction of an author's chair, in which students read their writing out loud to their classmates.

Although the phonetic spelling or invented spelling that primary students employ in these early stages may not be the conventional spelling of certain words, it allows primary students to practice the art and flow of writing. It works to build their confidence in the writing process. This is not the time for educators to correct spelling, punctuation, or capitalization errors, as young learners may quickly lose interest in writing and may lose self-confidence.

One strategy to employ early on to help students with proper spelling is to ensure there is an easily accessible and updated word wall that employs high-frequency words and sight words. Students should be encouraged to refer to the word wall while they write.

Usage
Usage concerns itself with word order, verb tense, and subject-verb agreement among other areas. As primary children often have a basic knowledge of how to use oral language effectively in order to communicate, this area of spelling conventions may require less initial attention than the mechanics of spelling. During read-aloud and shared reading activities, educators may wish to point out punctuation marks found in print, model how to read these punctuation marks, and periodically discuss their importance in the reading and writing process.

When children begin to engage in writing exercises, educators may wish to prompt self-editing skills by asking if each sentence begins with a capital and ends with a period, question mark, or exclamation point.

<u>Sentence Formation</u>   *Parts of Speech*

Verbs, nouns, adverbs, and adjectives all play significant roles in the writing process. However, for primary students, these concepts are fairly complex to understand. One instruction approach that may prove effective is to categorize a number of simple verbs, nouns, adverbs, and adjectives on index cards by color coordination. Educators can then ask one child to choose a noun card and another student to choose a verb card. The children can then face the class and read their words starting with the noun and then the verb. The students can even try reading the verb first followed by the noun. A class discussion can follow, analyzing whether or not the sentences made sense and what words might need to be added to give the sentence more meaning.

Skills in Using Phonics

Instruction of phonics skills and sight words for students with reading difficulties, disabilities, or special needs should be streamlined, systematic, and explicit. Focus should be committed toward essential skills and the highest-frequency sight words. Phonics skills and sight words that are lacking and words that are often misspelled need to be targeted through remediation and routine practice. Concepts and tasks should be supported through the employment of a variety of concrete examples. Visual, auditory, kinesthetic, and tactile techniques, such as the multisensory writing strategies previously discussed, will help to promote spelling and mastery of new sight words.

Instruction of phonics skills, sight word knowledge, and the spelling of single-syllable words can also be differentiated for ELLs and speakers of nonstandard English. For these students, teachers ought to capitalize on the transfer of relevant knowledge, skills, and similar words from a student's primary language into the English language. In this way, extra attention and instructional emphasis can be applied toward the teaching of sounds and meanings of words that are nontransferable between the two languages.

Advanced learners benefit from phonics skills, sight word knowledge, and spelling of single-syllable words of increased complexity. The breadth of current knowledge and skills ought to be extended for advanced learners, and instruction should occur at a faster pace.

Word-Analysis Skills and Vocabulary Development

Phonics and Word Analysis

Phonics is the study of sound-letter relationships in alphabetic writing systems, such as the English language, and it is paramount to a child's future ability to read and write. Phonics helps children recognize and identify letter symbols and translate these symbols into their corresponding sound units, phonemes. The study of phonics concerns itself with the *Alphabetic Principle*—the systematic relationships that exist between letters and sounds—as well as with *Phonemic Awareness*—the understanding that letters correspond with distinct sounds and that there are specific rules governing the placement of letters in the English language.

As children become more familiar with recognizing the names and shapes of each letter, called *graphemes*, they begin to verbally practice their corresponding sounds—the phonemes. Although this sounds straightforward, it can pose significant challenges to both the children and teachers.

For example, when children learn that the letter *y* is pronounced /wigh/, but that it can make other various sounds, including /ee/, /i/, and /igh/—depending on letter placement—it may take repeated practice in order for children to pronounce and read this one letter accurately. Some examples would be the words, *happy, gym,* and *cry.* Although each word contains the same vowel, *y,* the placement of the *y* in each word differs, which affects the letter's pronunciation.

For this reason, there is an ongoing debate in literacy circles regarding the appropriate instructional approach for teaching phonics. Should educators teach letter shapes with their corresponding names or letter shapes with their corresponding sound or sounds? Is it possible to combine instruction to include shapes, names, and sounds, or should each of these skills be taught in isolation with a cumulative approach—shape, sound/s, and name? Some experts believe that when children are introduced to letter names and shapes in isolation of their corresponding sounds, children can become quickly confused, which can delay reading acquisition. Therefore, the answer to what approach to take lies with a keen understanding of a student's background knowledge in English and each child's specific needs. In order to create effective phonics instruction and help students strengthen literacy development, it is strongly suggested that educators are sensitive and aware of these unique challenges to English language acquisition.

It is widely accepted that letter-sound relationships are best taught systematically, introducing one relationship at a time and gradually increasing in complexity. Effective instruction in the initial stages of phonics awareness involves explicit introduction of the most important and the most frequently used letter-sound relationships. For instance, short vowels should be introduced and practiced ahead of long vowels, and lower-case letters should be introduced ahead of upper case as they occur the most often. Letters that frequently appear in simple words, such as /a/, /m/, and /t/ would be logical starting points, followed by letters that look similar but carry different sounds, as in /b/ and /d/.

The following guide offers an introduction of phonics instruction:

Introduction	Examples
Initial consonants	s, t, m, n, p
Short vowel and consonant	-it, -in, -at, -an
Consonant blends	-st, -bl, -dr
Digraphs	-th, -ph, -sh, -ch
Long vowels	ear, eat, oar, oat
Final (silent) e	site, mine, lane
Variant vowels and diphthongs	-au, -oo, -ow, -ou, -oi
Silent letters and inflectional endings	-kn, -gn, -wr, es, s

Effective phonics instruction begins with focusing on the overall literacy experiences of the students and connecting these experiences to further their literacy development. Best practices in teaching will work to establish a student's prior phonics knowledge, if there is any at all. Educators can differentiate their instruction based on their students' unique needs and background knowledge of phonics. Creating phonics activities that ensure students are actively engaged and motivated is key to overall success in literacy development.

Once children have mastered the relationship that exists between the names, shapes, sounds of letters, and letter combinations, educators may begin a more implicit instructional approach by incorporating the children's current phonics awareness with simple basal readers that focus on basic monosyllabic words. Grouping monosyllabic words according to their initial sounds continues to be an effective approach to instruction as the students advance in their understanding and application of phonics. When educators combine or further this practice with that of identifying the names of the initial letters in the words, children are likely to have more success with overall literacy development. A word wall with simple consonant-vowel-consonant words in alphabetical order acts as a visual reference to help strengthen a child's literacy development:

Word Wall

A	B	C
add	ball	car
age	bean	clean
ant	black	cub

At this stage, educators begin laying the foundation for reading readiness. Children begin listening to others read and start to recognize familiar sounds within the words being read. They independently practice sounding out words and will soon learn how to independently segment, blend, and manipulate the individual sounds in each newly acquired word.

When a child demonstrates phonological awareness and a clear understanding of how phonics works, they are ready to further their literacy development with *word analysis*. Word analysis is an effective study that helps students acquire new vocabulary. *Morphemes* are when words are broken down into their smallest units of meaning. Each morpheme within words carry specific meanings, therefore adding to children's understanding of entire words. When children begin to recognize key morphemes—especially prefixes and suffixes—they are beginning to demonstrate word analysis skills, which is a critical foundation in literacy development.

Word analysis helps children to read and comprehend complex reading materials, including informational texts. It is essential for vocabulary development. Word analysis skills also help children clarify the meaning of unknown words, figurative language, word relationships, and nuances in word meaning with the use of context clues.

Some effective instructional strategies to teach word analysis skills include Universal Design for Learning (UDL), studying words according to a subject theme, using diagrams and graphic organizers, and pre-teaching and reviewing new vocabulary on a regular basis. UDL involves the modeling of how to analyze new words by breaking them down into their individual morphemes and studying each morpheme separately. Once each morpheme in a given word has been identified and defined, students put the morphemes back together in order to understand the word in its entirety. The following is a word analysis study of the word *astronaut*:

Word	Morpheme 1	Morpheme 2	Word Meaning
astronaut	astro—Greek origin, roughly translates to anything relating to the stars and outer space	naut—Greek origin, roughly translates to "sailor"	a sailor of outer space

Studying words according to a shared theme is another effective word analysis strategy. For instance, when studying mathematics, educators may focus on words that contain the same prefix, such as *kilometer*, *kilogram*, and *kilowatt*. Common suffixes in science include *microscope*, *telescope*, and *macroscope*.

Diagrams and graphic organizers provide students with visual clues to contrast and compare word meanings. From organizational charts and mind maps to Venn diagrams and more, visual aids help students readily see and analyze the similarities and differences in various word meanings.

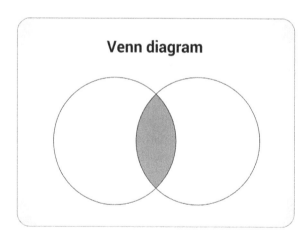

With the introduction to new topics of discussion or a new theme to any subject area, it is likely that there will also be an introduction to new, unfamiliar words. Both educators and students will benefit from a formal introduction to these new words prior to the lesson. Pre-teaching new vocabulary increases vocabulary acquisition and allows children to become comfortable and familiar with new terms ahead of the lesson. Pre-teaching new vocabulary has also been shown to reduce unnecessary stress and time that would otherwise be taken to stop lessons in order to explain unfamiliar words.

How Phonics, Syntax, and Semantics Interact

Vocabulary
Vocabulary consists of the bank of words that children can understand and apply fluently in order to communicate effectively. A strong vocabulary and word recognition base enables children to access

prior knowledge and experiences in order to make connections in written texts. A strong vocabulary also allows children to express ideas, learn new concepts, and decode the meanings of unfamiliar words by using context clues. Conversely, if a child's vocabulary knowledge is limited and does not steadily increase, reading comprehension will be negatively affected. If children become frustrated with their lack of understanding of written texts, they will likely choose to only read texts at their comfort level or refuse to read altogether. With direct instruction, educators introduce specific words to pre-teach before reading, or examine word roots, prefixes, and suffixes. Through indirect instruction, educators ensure that students are regularly exposed to new words. This engages students in high-quality conversations and social interactions and provides access to a wide variety of challenging and enjoyable reading material.

Morphology

The study of **morphology** generally deals with the structure and formation of words. A **phoneme** is the smallest unit of sound that does not necessarily carry meaning. Essentially, phonemes are combined to form words, and words are combined to form sentences. Morphology looks at the smallest meaningful part of a word, known as a **morpheme**. In contrast to a phoneme, a morpheme must carry a sound and a meaning. Free morphemes are those that can stand alone, carrying both sound and meaning, as in the following words: *girl, boy, man,* and *lady.* Just as the name suggests, **bound morphemes** are bound to other morphemes in order to carry meaning. Examples of bound morphemes include: *ish, ness, ly,* and *dis.*

Semantics

Semantics is the branch of linguistics that addresses meanings. Morphemes, words, phrases, and sentences all carry distinct meanings. The way these individual parts are arranged can have a significant effect on meaning. In order to construct language, children must be able to use semantics to arrange and rearrange words to achieve the particular meaning they are striving for. Activities that teach semantics revolve around teaching the arrangement of word parts (morphology) and root words, and then the teaching of vocabulary. Moving from vocabulary words into studying sentences and sentence structure leads children to learn how to use context clues to determine meaning and to understand anomalies such as metaphors, idioms, and allusions.

There are five types of semantic relationships that are critical to understand:

- **Hyponyms** refer to a relationship between words where general words have multiple more-specific words (hyponyms) that fall into the same category (e.g., horse: mare, stallion, foal, Appaloosa, Clydesdale).

- **Meronyms** refer to a relationship between words where a whole word has multiple parts (meronyms) that comprise it (e.g., horse: tail, mane, hooves, ears).

- **Synonyms** refer to words that have the same meaning as another word (e.g., instructor/teacher/educator, canine/dog, feline/cat, herbivore/vegetarian).

- Antonyms refer to words that have the opposite meaning as another word (e.g., true/false, up/down, in/out, right/wrong).

- **Homonyms** refer to words that are spelled the same (homographs) or sound the same (**homophones**) but mean different things (e.g., there/their/they're, two/too/to, principal/principle, plain/plane, (kitchen) sink/ sink (down as in water)).

Syntax

With its origins from the Greek word, "syntaxis," which means arrangement, **syntax** is the study of phrase and sentence formation. The study of syntax focuses on the ways in which specific words can be combined to create coherent meaning. For example: the simple rearrangement of the words, "I can run," is different from the question, "Can I run?" which is also different from the meaningless "Run I can."

The following methods can be used to teach syntax:

- Proper Syntax Modeling: Students don't need to be corrected for improper syntax. Instead, they should be shown ways to rephrase what they said with proper syntax. If a student says, "Run I can," then the teacher should say, "Oh, you can run how fast?" This puts syntax in place with conversational skills.

- Open-Ended Sentences: Students can complete open-ended sentences with proper syntax both orally and in written format, or they can correct sentences that have improper syntax so that they make sense.

- Listening for Syntax: Syntax is auditory. Students can often hear a syntax error before they can see it in writing. Teachers should have students use word cards or word magnets to arrange and rearrange simple sentences and read them aloud to check for syntax.

- Repetition: Syntax can be practiced by using songs, poems, and rhymes for repetitive automation.

Pragmatics

Pragmatics is the study of what words mean in certain situations. It helps to understand the intentions and interpretations of intentions through words used in human interaction. Different listeners and different situations call for different language and intonations of language. When people engage in a conversation, it is usually to convey a certain message, and the message (even using the same words) can change depending on the setting and the audience. The more fluent the speaker, the more success she or he will have in conveying the intended message.

The following methods can be used to teach pragmatics:

- When students state something incorrectly, a response can be given to what they intended to say in the first place. For instance, if a student says, "That's how it didn't happen." Then the teacher might say, "Of course, that's not how it happened." Instead of putting students on defense by being corrected, this method puts them at ease and helps them learn.

- Role-playing conversations with different people in different situations can help teach pragmatics. For example, pretend playing can be used where a situation remains the same but the audience changes, or the audience stays the same but the situations change. This can be followed with a discussion about how language and intonations change too.

- Different ways to convey a message can be used, such as asking vs. persuading, or giving direct vs. indirect requests and polite vs. impolite messages.

- Various non-verbal signals can be used to see how they change pragmatics. For example, students can be encouraged to use mismatched words and facial expressions, such as angry words while smiling or happy words while pretending to cry.

Strategies to Help Read New and/or Difficult Words

Children who are developing reading fluency and comprehension skills can become frustrated when presented with unfamiliar words in a given text. With direct phonics instruction, educators can teach children to decode words and then use context clues to define the words while reading. If children have a strong enough understanding of language structures, including nouns and verbs, educators can ask them to consider what part of speech the unknown word might be based on and where it might fit into the sentence. Other useful strategies involve **self-monitoring**, in which children are asked to think as they read and ask themselves if what they have just read makes sense. Focusing on visual clues, such as drawings and photographs, may give children valuable insight into deciphering unknown words. Looking for the word in another section of the text to see how it relates to the overall meaning could give a clue to the new vocabulary word. Spelling the word out loud or looking for word chunks, prefixes, and suffixes, as well as demonstrating how to segment the unknown word into its individual syllables, may also be effective strategies to employ.

One of the most valuable strategies, however, for helping children to read and understand new words is **pre-teaching**. In this strategy, educators select what they evaluate to be the unfamiliar words in the text and then introduce them to the class before reading. Educators using this method should be careful not to simply ask the children to read the text and then spell the new words correctly. They should also provide clear definitions and give the children the opportunity to read these words in various sentences to decipher word meaning. This method can dramatically reduce how often children stop reading in order to reflect on unknown words. Educators are often unsure as to whether to correct every mispronounced word a child makes when reading. If the mispronounced word still makes sense, it is sometimes better to allow the child to continue to read, since the more the child stops, the more the child's reading comprehension and fluency are negatively affected.

Word-Analysis Skills

Phonics and decoding skills aid the analysis of new words. **Word analysis** is the ability to recognize the relationships between the spelling, syllabication, and pronunciation of new and/or unfamiliar words. Having a clear understanding of word structure, orthography, and the meaning of morphemes also aid in the analysis of new words.

However, not all words follow predictable phonics patterns, morphology, or orthography. Such irregular words must be committed to memory and are called sight words.

Phonics skills, syllabic skills, structural analysis, word analysis, and memorization of sight words lead to word recognition automaticity. **Word recognition** is the ability to correctly and automatically recognize words in or out of context. Word recognition is a prerequisite for fluent reading and reading comprehension.

Reading Multisyllabic Words by Using Syllabication and Structural Analysis

Reading competence of multisyllabic words is accomplished through phonics skills that are accompanied with a reader's ability to recognize morphological structures within words. **Structural analysis** is a word recognition skill that focuses on the meaning of word parts, or morphemes, during the introduction of a new word. Therefore, the instruction of structural analysis focuses on the recognition and application of morphemes. **Morphemes** are word parts such as base words, prefixes, inflections, and suffixes. Students can use structural analysis skills to find familiar word parts within an unfamiliar word in order to decode the word and determine the definition of the new word. Identification and association of such word segments also aids the proper pronunciation and spelling of new multisyllabic words.

Similarly, learning to apply phonics skills to longer and more complex words relies on a reader's ability to recognize syllable structures within multisyllabic words. **Syllabic analysis**, or **syllabication**, is a word analysis skill that helps students split words into syllables. **Syllables** are phonological units that contain a vowel sound. Students may be intimidated by long, multisyllabic words. Helping students break up multisyllabic words into morphological units (structural analysis) and phonological units according to syllable types makes longer words appear as a connected series of smaller words. The identified syllables can then be blended, pronounced, and/or written together as a single word. This helps students learn to decode and encode the longer words more accurately and efficiently with less anxiety. Thus, syllabic analysis leads to the rapid word recognition that is critical in reading fluency and comprehension.

The following table identifies the six basic syllable patterns that should be explicitly taught during syllabic instruction:

Basic Syllable Patterns		
Name of Syllable Type	Characteristics of Syllable Type	Examples
Closed	A syllable with a single vowel closed in by a consonant.	lab, bog, an
Open	A syllable that ends with a single vowel. Note that the letter *y* acts as a vowel.	go, me, sly
Vowel-Consonant-Silent *e*	A syllable with a single vowel followed by a consonant then *e*.	like, rake, note, obese
Vowel Teams	A syllable that has two consecutive vowels. Note that the letters *w* and *y* act as vowels.	meat, pertain, bay, toad, window
R-controlled	A syllable with one or two vowels followed by the letter *r*.	car, jar, fir, sir, collar, turmoil

Basic Syllable Patterns		
Consonant le (-al, -el) Also called final stable	A syllable that has a consonant followed by the letters le, al, or el.	puddle, stable, uncle, bridal, pedal
Other final stable syllables	A syllable at the end of words can be taught as a recognizable unit such as cious, age, ture, tion, or sion.	pension, elation, puncture, stumpage, fictitious

Context Clues

Reference materials are the most obvious way students can independently learn the definition and pronunciation of new vocabulary terms.

When using **contextual strategies**, students are introduced to new words indirectly within a sentence or paragraph. Contextual strategies require students to infer the meaning of a word by utilizing semantic and contextual clues.

The use of appositives and parenthetical elements can be very effective contextual strategies. **Appositives** are words or a group of words that add meaning or define a term that directly precedes them. An example of a sentence that includes apposition is: "Strawberries, heart-shaped and red berries, are delicious when eaten right off of the vine." In this sentence, the definition of strawberries ("heart shaped and red berries") directly follows the term and is introduced with and closes with a comma. **Parenthetical elements** are specific types of appositives that add details to a term but not necessarily a definition. For example: "My cat, the sweetest in the whole world, didn't come home last night." In this sentence, the parenthetical element ("the sweetest in the whole world") further describes the cat but does not provide a definition of the word "cat."

Structural analysis skills are beneficial in the pronunciation of new words. When readers use **structural analysis**, they recognize affixes or roots as meaningful word parts within a word. When a new word doesn't contain parts that are recognized by a student, the reader can use phonic letter–sound patterns to divide the word into syllables. The word parts can then be combined to yield the proper pronunciation.

Word maps are visual organizers that promote structural analysis skills for vocabulary development. **Word maps** may require students to define or provide synonyms, antonyms, and pictures for given vocabulary terms. Alternatively, **morphological maps** may be used to relate words that share a common morpheme.

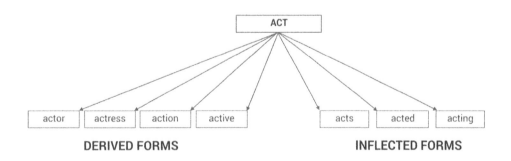

DERIVED FORMS   INFLECTED FORMS

Similarly, **word webs** are used to compare and classify a list of words. Word webs show relationships between new words and a student's background knowledge. With the main concept placed centrally within the word web, secondary and tertiary terms stem off from this central concept.

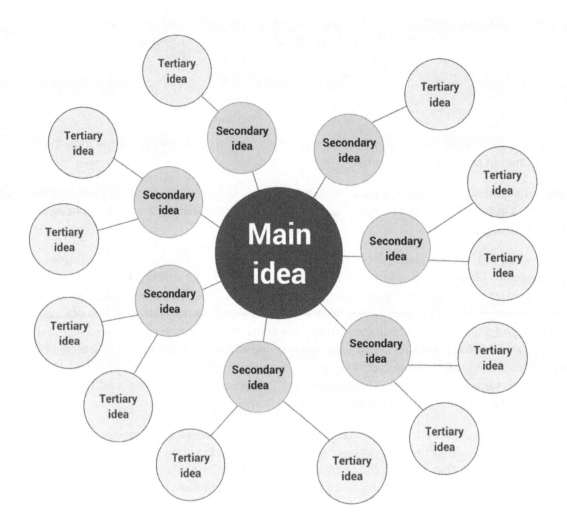

The table below identifies additional ways in which teachers can help students independently define unfamiliar words or words with multiple meanings:

Strategy	Examples
By Definition: Look up the word in a dictionary or thesaurus. Helps students realize that a single word can have multiple meanings.	Her favorite fruit to eat was a date. He went on a date with his girlfriend.
By Example: Invite students to offer their own examples, or to state their understanding following your own examples.	A myth is a story attempting to explain a natural phenomenon, such as the story of Prometheus to understand fire.
By Synonym: Understand that words have many different meanings. Some words are better synonyms than others.	She was very happy that day; her face was *radiant* with joy.
By Antonym: Teach student to look for words that have opposite meanings if the context of the sentence calls for its opposite.	Hannah was not happy that day; she was, in fact, very *depressed*.
By Apposition: **Apposition** is when the definition is given within the sentence.	The mango, a round, yellow, juicy fruit with an enormous seed in the middle, was ripe enough to eat.
By Origin: Identify Greek and Latin roots to figure out meanings of words.	In the word *hypertension*, the root *"hyper"* is a Greek word meaning "above" or "over."
By Context: Identifying what a word means by the surrounding text.	Water evaporates when it becomes hot, and the liquid turns into gas.

Vocabulary Knowledge

Vocabulary knowledge is an indicator and predictor of comprehension. If students find a match between a word within a text and a word that they've learned through listening and speaking, they are likelier to recognize and understand the meaning of the word in the written context. As the students will spend less time decoding and interpreting the word, they are likelier to read fluently and with comprehension. In contrast, if students cannot connect a written word to a word within their speaking or listening vocabulary, their fluency and comprehension may be interrupted. This proves to be true even if the student is able to correctly pronounce the word.

Word-Reference Materials

Reference materials are indispensable tools for beginners and experts alike. Becoming a competent English communicator doesn't necessarily mean memorizing every single rule about spelling, grammar, or punctuation; rather, it means knowing where and how to find accurate information about the rules of English usage. Students of English have a wide variety of references materials available to them, and, in an increasingly digitized world, more and more of these materials can be found online or as easily-accessible phone applications. Educators should introduce students to different types of reference materials as well as when and how to use them.

Spell Check

Most word processing software programs come equipped with a spell-checking feature. Web browsers and personal devices like smartphones and tablets may also have a spell checker enabled. **Spell check** automatically detects misspelled words and suggests alternate spellings. Many writers have come to rely on spell check due to its convenience and ease of use. However, there are some caveats to using spell check—it only checks whether a word is spelled correctly, not if it is used correctly. As discussed above, there are numerous examples of commonly-confused words in English, the misuse of which may not be detected by a spell checker. Many word processing programs do integrate spell checking and grammar checking functions, however. Thus, although running a spell check is an important part of reviewing any piece of writing, it should not be the only step of the review process. Further, spell checkers recommend correctly-spelled words based on an approximation of the misspelled word, so writers need to be somewhat close to the correct spelling in order for spell check to be useful.

Dictionary

Dictionaries are readily available in print, digital formats, and as mobile apps. A dictionary offers a wealth of information to users. First, in the absence of spell checking software, a **dictionary** can be used to identify correct spelling and to determine the word's pronunciation—often written using the International Phonetic Alphabet (IPA). Perhaps the best-known feature of a dictionary is its explanation of a word's meanings as a single word can have multiple definitions. A dictionary organizes these definitions based on their parts of speech and then arranges them from most to least commonly used meanings or from oldest to most modern usage. Many dictionaries also offer information about a word's etymology and usage. With all these functions, then, a dictionary is a basic, essential tool in many situations. Students can turn to a dictionary when they encounter an unfamiliar word or when they see a familiar word used in a new way.

There are many dictionaries to choose from, but perhaps the most highly respected source is the *Oxford English Dictionary* (OED). The OED is a historical dictionary, and as such, all entries include quotes of the word as it has been used throughout history. Users of the OED can get a deeper sense of a word's evolution over time and in different parts of the world. Another standard dictionary in America is *Merriam-Webster*.

Thesaurus

Whereas a dictionary entry lists a word's definitions, a **thesaurus** entry lists a word's **synonyms** and **antonyms**—i.e., words with similar and opposite meanings, respectively. A dictionary can be used to find out what a word means and where it came from, and a thesaurus can be used to understand a word's relationship to other words. A thesaurus can be a powerful vocabulary-building tool. By becoming familiar with synonyms and antonyms, students will be more equipped to use a broad range of vocabulary in their speech and writing. Of course, one thing to be aware of when using a thesaurus is that most words do not have exact synonyms. Rather, there are slight nuances of meaning that can make one word more appropriate than another in a given context. In this case, it is often to the user's advantage to consult a thesaurus side-by-side with a dictionary to confirm any differences in usage between two synonyms. Some digital sources, such as *Dictionary.com*, integrate a dictionary and a thesaurus.

Generally, though, a thesaurus is a useful tool to help writers add variety and precision to their word choice. Consulting a thesaurus can help students elevate their writing to an appropriate academic level by replacing vague or overused words with more expressive or academic ones. Also, word processors often offer a built-in thesaurus, making it easy for writers to look up synonyms and vary word choice as they work.

Glossary

A **glossary** is similar to a dictionary in that it offers an explanation of terms. However, while a dictionary attempts to cover every word in a language, a glossary only focuses on those terms relevant to a specific field. Also, a glossary entry is more likely to offer a longer explanation of a term and its relevance within that field. Glossaries are often found at the back of textbooks or other nonfiction publications in order to explain new or unfamiliar terms to readers. A glossary may also be an entire book on its own that covers all of the essential terms and concepts within a particular profession, field, or other specialized area of knowledge. Thus, for learners seeking general definitions of terms from any context, a dictionary is an appropriate reference source, but for students of specialized fields, a glossary will usually provide more in-depth information.

Style Manual

Many rules of English usage are standard, but other rules may be more subjective. An example can be seen in the following structures:

A. I went to the store and bought eggs, milk, and bread.
B. I went to the store and bought eggs, milk and bread.

The final comma in a list before *and* or *or* is known as an **Oxford comma** or **serial comma**. It is recommended in some styles, but not in others. To determine the appropriate use of the Oxford comma, writers can consult a style manual.

A **style manual** is a comprehensive collection of guidelines for language use and document formatting. Some fields refer to a common style guide—e.g., the Associated Press or *AP Stylebook*, a standard in American journalism. Individual organizations may rely on their own house style. Regardless, the purpose of a style manual is to ensure uniformity across all documents. Style manuals explain things such as how to format titles, when to write out numbers or use numerals, and how to cite sources. Because there are many different style guides, students should know how and when to consult an appropriate guide. *The Chicago Manual of Style* is common in the publication of books and academic journals. The Modern Language Association style (MLA) is another commonly used academic style format, while the American Psychological Association style (APA) may be used for scientific publications. Familiarity with using a style guide is particularly important for students who are college bound or pursuing careers in academic or professional writing.

In the examples above, the Oxford comma is recommended by the Chicago Manual of Style, so sentence A would be correct if the writer is using this style. But the comma is not recommended by the *AP Stylebook*, so sentence B would be correct if the writer is using the AP style.

General Grammar and Style References

Any language arts textbook should offer general grammatical and stylistic advice to students, but there are a few well-respected texts that can also be used for reference. *Elements of Style* by William Strunk is regularly assigned to students as a guide on effective written communication, including how to avoid common usage mistakes and how to make the most of parallel structure. *Garner's Modern American Usage* by Bryan Garner is another text that guides students on how to achieve precision and understandability in their writing. Whereas other reference sources discussed above tend to address specific language concerns, these types of texts offer a more holistic approach to cultivating effective language skills.

With print texts, it is easy to identify the authors and their credentials, as well as the publisher and their reputation. With electronic resources like websites, though, it can be trickier to assess the reliability of information. Students should be alert when gathering information from the Internet. Understanding the significance of website **domains**—which include identification strings of a site—can help. Website domains ending in *.edu* are educational sites and tend to offer more reliable research in their field. A *.org* ending tends to be used by nonprofit organizations and other community groups, *.com* indicates a privately-owned website, and a *.gov* site is run by the government. Websites affiliated with official organizations, research groups, or institutes of learning are more likely to offer relevant, fact-checked, and reliable information.

Development of Reading Fluency and Reading Comprehension

Automatic Word Recognition, Accuracy, and Prosody for Reading Fluency

Word recognition occurs when students are able to correctly and automatically recognize and read a word. Phonics and sight word instruction help with the promotion of accurate and automatic word identification and word recognition. Once students are able to readily identify and recognize words, their attention is not devoted toward the dissection of word interpretation, and they can focus on the meaning of the text, supporting reading comprehension skills.

Phonics instruction stresses letter-sound correspondences and the manipulation of phonemes. Through phonics instruction, students learn the relationships between the letters and symbols of written language and the sounds of spoken language. It is through the application of phonics principles that students are able to decode words. When a word is **decoded,** the letters that make up the printed word are translated into sounds. When students are able to recognize and manipulate letter-sound relationships of single-syllable words, they are able to apply such relationships to decode more complex words. In this way, phonics aids reading fluency and reading comprehension.

Sight words, sometimes referred to as **high-frequency words**, are words that are used often but may not follow the regular principles of phonics. Sight words may also be defined as words that students are able to readily recognize and read without having to sound them out. Students are encouraged to memorize words by sight so their reading fluency is not deterred through the frequent decoding of regularly- occurring irregular words. In this way, sight word recognition aids reading fluency and reading comprehension.

Accuracy, Rate, and Prosody
In order to understand the objectives of RICA's Domain 3, the following three key indicators of reading fluency must be understood:

- *Accuracy* refers to the correct reading and pronunciation of words.

- *Reading rate* refers to the speed at which an individual reads within a given amount of time, often measured in words per minute.

- *Prosody* refers to the appropriate use of expression, intonation, emphasis, and tone when reading.

As word recognition increases, readers become less taxed with the interpretation of a text; thus, reading fluency and comprehension improve. When students read too quickly or too slowly for their skill level, they may lose reading comprehension. As accuracy and fluency increase, students begin to read aloud with appropriate prosody, and reading becomes a natural process.

Linguistic, Sociological, Cultural, Cognitive, and Psychological Bases of the Reading Process

Much of a student's reading comprehension will be influenced by their individual perspective and upbringing. Cultural and social values inform the way children think from a young age, and these factors play a major role in their cognition and psychological development. Therefore, it's important to understand that some students, including those learning English as a second language, may not interpret reading the way a typical native English speaker would. The role of the teacher is to be respectful and receptive of students' understanding of reading and guide them in drawing correct analysis. Being mindful of cultural differences will enable instructors to understand how their students think, or at least help identify any disconnects, to tailor instruction appropriately.

Different cultures may not share some of the values, goals, or general views Americans share. For example, Americans tend to be skeptical of and question leadership, yet another culture might put trust more easily in leadership and find questioning authority to be counterproductive or seditious. This alternate view of the subject matter may result in difficulty understanding the concepts when reading a passage on such a topic. It's important to remember that, although outside and individual views are not wrong, students should be able to draw an accurate analysis of reading content. Reading confusion can be avoided through simple, yet thorough, linguistic training.

Instructors should strive to focus on basic rules of English. Students must know how English works and sounds before they can connect meaning to sentences. Again, each student learns differently, so individualized instruction might be needed to help students who are having issues with the material. This approach is also known as **scaffolding**.

The **input hypothesis of language learning** suggests that students can make breakthroughs in language comprehension when they are exposed to material slightly above their current level. It's important not to overwhelm students but to be patient with them through complex material; the result will be that they can read and understand a variety of other texts after mastering difficult reading concepts. However, if the material is too difficult, easier reading may be substituted.

Reading Comprehension Strategies

Organizational/Explanatory Features
Using and understanding references is imperative in developing reading comprehension skills. Pre-teaching a lesson on understanding references can be helpful, or a teacher may even incorporate this skill into teaching some broader comprehension skills. Prior to teaching from the basal reader, or prior to each story in the basal reader, a teacher should address the table of contents at the beginning of the textbook. This teaches students to use the table of contents frequently and allows them to find parts of a story that they will be reading on their own. When teaching from nonfiction texts, such as social studies or science, instruction should be provided on using the index to identify and locate specific information to answer comprehension questions. Both nonfiction and fiction texts can be used to teach how to use the glossary to locate boldfaced and important vocabulary. It is often most beneficial to identify and teach new vocabulary prior to reading a piece, so that students gain a deeper understanding of the text as they read it for the first time.

<u>Typographic Features</u>
Understanding changes in the appearance of text will help students easily identify important information. Pointing out boldfaced words during reading instruction tells students these may be important words in the understanding of the text, and that new vocabulary may be present. Boldfacing or italics may help students identify when a thought or topic is changing or being brought to attention. Color-coding may be used when comparing or contrasting different parts of the text. During reading comprehension instruction time, it is important to point out when these changes occur. It is also helpful to try to find text of this nature to use in small group or whole group instruction. Text with these types of typographic features assist students on their path to reading comprehension.

<u>Graphic Features</u>
Graphics always help interpret a story or text. Younger learners rely on pictures to help tell the story, while older students use diagrams, maps, and charts to aid in understanding texts. Even for adults, graphic features assist with visualizing the text being read. Charts and diagrams help organize information into more clear and concise patterns. Maps help understand specific places and locations. Illustrations help visualize a fictional story. Furthermore, illustrations with captions help visualize nonfiction and fiction texts, particularly when paired with captions that provide an explanation of why the illustration is important.

Independent Reading in the Development of Reading Comprehension and Fluency

Independent reading strategies promote healthy reading for pleasure and enjoyment. Hopefully, these strategies promote a lifelong love of reading. Students should be given daily, independent reading time in the classroom. Teachers phrase this time as **D.E.A.R.** or "Drop Everything and Read" time. Typically, this time can be incorporated into a teacher's reading block. It is suggested that students have about 20 minutes of D.E.A.R. time daily. Students can read a book from home, the library, or one selected from the variety of books found within the classroom.

Promoting Independent Reading

Teachers are required to have a classroom library. Some schools require a certain number of books or filled bookcases within a classroom. The library center should also contain more than just books. The classroom library should be an inviting environment for students. Small lamps make the area warmer—like home rather than school—and provide extra light for reading. Furniture—such as beanbag chairs, pillows, and small chairs—allow students to get comfortable, rather than reading at their desk. Not only is the environment important, but the reading center must also be an organized, designated space. If books are disorganized in the classroom library, students may be deterred from using the space appropriately, simply because they cannot find what they are looking for, or out of shear frustration. Organizing books by theme or genre helps students search for the books they desire. For students in younger grades, books should be grouped in plastic tubs using picture and word category labels like "animals" or "holidays." This organization method is especially helpful to those learning to read.

A listening center is also another helpful space in the classroom library. In the listening center, students listen to stories that are played through a sound device (like a CD or MP3 player) and follow along in the text. A teacher can switch the book out weekly to match a theme in the classroom, or can leave a "free choice bin" for students to choose what they would like to listen to. Again, listening to the story will encourage and emphasize reading strategies, such as voice and pacing.

Having a bookshelf with the teacher's or students' text selections may encourage readers to select a good book quickly. Some students enjoy re-reading a book from a teacher read aloud; therefore, placing it in the "teacher's pick" area may encourage developing readers to pick it up. Students also like to follow their classmates. Therefore, teachers should have a section where students can place a book that students can recommend to their friends. For older students, brief recommendation sheets can be filled out by the students. These sheets briefly list a few of a book's main themes so that potential readers can see if they are interested in reading the book. Reading from basal readers and school texts do not necessarily encourage reading for pleasure, as they are texts that are chosen by the school and instructor. For this reason, silent reading time is so important. Silent reading time gives students options and a chance to make their own choices. Students can choose the book and the appropriate reading pace when reading independently.

Promoting Family and Community Involvement in Literacy Activities

The following are strategies for promoting purposeful and independent reading of a wide variety of texts:

- Promote independent reading of narrative, literary, expository, and informational texts.
- Teach students how to select books that are at appropriate reading levels.
- Use students' personal interests to help motivate them to read independently.
- Provide structured reading opportunities in class.
- Encourage independent reading at home.
- Monitor students' independent reading.

In addition to teacher read-alouds, as discussed earlier, students should have approximately twenty minutes per day to read independently. This time should be structured and occur at predictable times each day or throughout the week. Students should be encouraged to read a variety of texts at this time (narrative, literary, expository, and informational texts). Students also should read independently.

In order to benefit from independent reading, students must read texts that are appropriate for their assessed reading level. Therefore, students should be aware of their reading levels and be able to select texts that coincide with this level. For students in primary school, the **five-finger test** can be used in the text-selection process. The five-finger test asserts that if a student has trouble with five or more words on a randomly selected page, then the book is above that student's reading level. For older readers, the teacher can group texts into levels and/or categories, from which students can select based on their personal interests.

In order for independent reading time to be effective, students should be accountable for what is read. A great assessment tool is to have each student give an oral report of one book that they have read during the marking period. Students should be given nightly reading homework as well. Teachers may require students to log the number of minutes read each night. Such reading logs should require parents to sign next to the number of minutes a night a child has read.

Reading Comprehension Strategies Across Text Types

Variety of Genres

Classifying literature involves an understanding of the concept of genre. A *genre* is a category of literature that possesses similarities in style and in characteristics. Based on form and structure, there are four basic genres.

Fictional Prose

Fictional prose consists of fictional works written in standard form with a natural flow of speech and without poetic structure. Fictional prose primarily utilizes grammatically complete sentences and a paragraph structure to convey its message.

Drama

Drama is fiction that is written to be performed in a variety of media, intended to be performed for an audience, and structured for that purpose. It might be composed using poetry or prose, often straddling the elements of both in what actors are expected to present. Action and dialogue are the tools used in drama to tell the story.

Poetry

Poetry is fiction in verse that has a unique focus on the rhythm of language and focuses on intensity of feeling. It is not an entire story, though it may tell one; it is compact in form and in function. Poetry can be considered as a poet's brief word picture for a reader. Poetic structure is primarily composed of lines and stanzas. Together, poetic structure and devices are the methods that poets use to lead readers to feeling an effect and, ultimately, to the interpretive message.

Literary Nonfiction

Literary nonfiction is prose writing that is based on current or past real events or real people and includes straightforward accounts as well as those that offer opinions on facts or factual events. The exam distinguishes between *literary nonfiction*—a form of writing that incorporates literary styles and techniques to create factually-based narratives—and informational texts, which will be addressed in the next section.

Independent and Reflective Reading

Students who engage in independent reading are able to read, retain, and analyze the text that they've read on their own, completely independent of outside aid. It also allows them to feel as if they've had a choice in picking their own text to read, instead of the feeling that it's been chosen for them. Reflective reading is the ability to absorb text with a sense of analysis in mind. Here are some examples of questions to ask while engaged in reflective reading:

- What am I reading?
- Why am I reading this?
- What is the author trying to tell me?
- Why is this character acting in a certain way?

Encouraging independent and reflective reading is dependent on the type of literature instructors choose to introduce to their classrooms. Culture, race, age, and reading level are all very important characteristics to keep in mind when choosing texts to have in the classroom for independent readers. If some students are ELLs, acquire some texts that are bilingual or ELL-appropriate. Choose authors with various ethnic backgrounds rather than the most popular books you find on an online blog. Find authors who have similar cultures to the students in the classroom. Choose difficult books for your advanced students and appropriate books for the students who still struggle with reading. Students will have a greater motivation to read and understand the language if they can relate to the message that's being delivered.

Literary Elements

There is no one, final definition of what literary elements are. They can be considered features or characteristics of fiction, but they are really more of a way that readers can unpack a text for the purpose of analysis and understanding the meaning. The elements contribute to a reader's literary interpretation of a passage as to how they function to convey the central message of a work. The most common literary elements used for analysis are the presented below.

Point of View

The *point of view* is the position the narrator takes when telling the story in prose. If a narrator is incorporated in a drama, the point of view may vary; in poetry, point of view refers to the position the speaker in a poem takes.

First Person

The first person point of view is when the writer uses the word "I" in the text. Poetry often uses first person, e.g., William Wordsworth's "I Wandered Lonely as a Cloud." Two examples of prose written in first person are Suzanne Collins' *The Hunger Games* and Anthony Burgess's *A Clockwork Orange*.

Second Person

The second person point of view is when the writer uses the pronoun "you." It is not widely used in prose fiction, but as a technique, it has been used by writers such as William Faulkner in *Absalom, Absalom!* and Albert Camus in *The Fall*. It is more common in poetry—e.g., Pablo Neruda's "If You Forget Me."

Third Person

Third person point of view is when the writer utilizes pronouns such as him, her, or them. It may be the most utilized point of view in prose as it provides flexibility to an author and is the one with which readers are most familiar. There are two main types of third person used in fiction. *Third person omniscient* uses a narrator that is all-knowing, relating the story by conveying and interpreting thoughts/feelings of all characters. In *third person limited,* the narrator relates the story through the perspective of one character's thoughts/feelings, usually the main character.

Plot

The *plot* is what happens in the story. Plots may be singular, containing one problem, or they may be very complex, with many sub-plots. All plots have exposition, a conflict, a climax, and a resolution. The *conflict* drives the plot and is something that the reader expects to be resolved. The plot carries those events along until there is a resolution to the conflict.

Tone

The *tone* of a story reflects the author's attitude and opinion about the subject matter of the story or text. Tone can be expressed through word choice, imagery, figurative language, syntax, and other details. The emotion or mood the reader experiences relates back to the tone of the story. Some examples of possible tones are humorous, somber, sentimental, and ironic.

Setting

The *setting* is the time, place, or set of surroundings in which the story occurs. It includes time or time span, place(s), climates, geography—man-made or natural—or cultural environments. Emily Dickinson's poem "Because I could not stop for Death" has a simple setting—the narrator's symbolic ride with Death through town towards the local graveyard. Conversely, Leo Tolstoy's *War and Peace* encompasses numerous settings within settings in the areas affected by the Napoleonic Wars, spanning 1805 to 1812.

Characters

Characters are the story's figures that assume primary, secondary, or minor roles. *Central* or *major* characters are those integral to the story—the plot cannot be resolved without them. A central character can be a *protagonist* or hero. There may be more than one protagonist, and he/she doesn't always have to possess good characteristics. A character can also be an *antagonist*—the force against a protagonist.

Dynamic characters change over the course of the plot time. *Static* characters do not change. A *symbolic* character is one that represents an author's idea about society in general—e.g., Napoleon in Orwell's *Animal Farm*. *Stock* characters are those that appear across genres and embrace stereotypes—e.g., the cowboy of the Wild West or the blonde bombshell in a detective novel. A *flat* character is one that does not present a lot of complexity or depth, while a *rounded* character does. Sometimes, the *narrator* of a story or the *speaker* in a poem can be a character—e.g., Nick Carraway in F. Scott Fitzgerald's *The Great Gatsby* or the speaker in Robert Browning's "My Last Duchess." The narrator might also function as a character in prose, though not be part of the story—e.g., Charles Dickens' narrator of *A Christmas Carol*.

How Variety of Genre Improves Comprehension

Reading is fundamental to learning. Reading nurtures imagination, critical thinking, communication skills, and social competence. Many children are drawn to the allure of reading and often their attention is captivated by a certain type of book or books about a particular personal interest. It is important to introduce them to an eclectic selection of text types. Cultural knowledge, a more intricate worldview, and a host of new vocabulary can be built through the experience of diverse literature. Reading a wide range of writing styles brings students into contact with many characters and lifestyles. Reading varied texts sparks different emotions in a child and teaches a variety of means of expression. In this way, children deepen social and emotional skills. In short, reading a wide variety of texts produces a well-rounded education and prepares children for their experience of the world.

Recognizing Various Genres in Literature

Fiction

Fiction is imaginative text that is invented by the author. Fiction is characterized by the following literary elements:

- **Characters:** the people, animals, aliens, or other living figures the story is about
- **Setting:** the location, surroundings, and time the story takes place in
- **Conflict:** a dilemma the characters face either internally or externally
- **Plot:** the sequence and the rise and fall of excitement in the action of a story
- **Resolution:** the solution to the conflict that is discovered as a result of the story
- **Point of View:** the lens through which the reader experiences the story
- **Theme:** the moral to the story or the message the author is sending to the reader

Historical Fiction

Historical fiction is a story that occurs in the past and uses a realistic setting and authentic time period characters. Historical fiction usually has some historically accurate events mixed and balanced with invented plot and characters.

Science Fiction
Science fiction is an invented story that occurs in the future or an alternate universe. It often deals with space, time travel, robots, or aliens, and highly-advanced technology.

Fantasy
Fantasy is a subgenre of fiction that involves magic or supernatural elements and/or takes place in an imaginary world. Examples include talking animals, superheroes rescuing the day, or characters taking on a mythical journey or quest.

Mystery and Adventure
Mystery fiction is a story that involves a puzzle or crime to be solved by the main characters. The mystery is driven by suspense and foreshadowing. The reader must sift through clues and distractions to solve the puzzle with the protagonist. **Adventure stories** are driven by the risky or exciting action that happens in the plot.

Realistic and Contemporary Fiction
Realistic fiction depends on the author portraying the world without speculation. The characters are ordinary, and the action could happen in real life. The conflict often involves growing up, family life, or learning to cope with some significant emotion or challenge.

Nonfiction Literature
Nonfiction literature is text that is true and accurate in detail. Nonfiction can cover virtually any topic in the natural world. Nonfiction writers conduct research and carefully organize facts before writing. Nonfiction has the following subgenres:

- **Informational Text:** This is text written to impart information to the reader. It may have literary elements such as charts, graphs, indexes, glossaries, or bibliographies.

- **Persuasive Text:** This is text that is meant to sway the reader to have a particular opinion or take a particular action.

- **Biographies and Autobiographies:** This is text that tells intimate details of someone's life. If an author writes the text about someone else, it is a **biography**. If the author writes it about himself or herself, it is an **autobiography.**

- **Communicative text:** This is text used to communicate with another person. This includes such texts as emails, formal and informal letters, and tweets. This content often consists of two-sided dialogue between people.

Drama
Drama is any writing that is intended to be performed in front of an audience, such as plays, and TV and movie scripts. Dialogue and action are central to convey the author's theme. **Comedy** is any drama designed to be funny or lighthearted. **Tragedy** is any drama designed to be serious or sad.

Poetry
This is text that is written in verse and has a rhythmic cadence. It often involves descriptive imagery, rhyming stanzas, and beautiful mastery of language. It is often personal, emotional, and introspective. Poetry is often considered a work of art.

<u>Folklore</u>
Folklore is literature that has been handed down from generation to generation by word of mouth. Folklore is not based in fact but in unsubstantiated beliefs. It is often very important to a culture or custom. The following are some common types of folklore:

- **Fairy Tales:** These are usually written for children and often carry a moral or universal truth. They are stories written about fairies or other magical creatures.

- **Fables:** Similar to fairy tales, fables are written for children and include tales of supernatural people or animals that speak like people. They often are built around a moral lesson.

- **Myths:** These tales are often about the gods, include symbolism, and may involve historical events and reveal human behavior. Sometimes they tell how historical things came about.

- **Legends:** Exaggerated and only partially truthful, these are tales of heroes and significant events.

- **Tall Tales:** Often funny stories and sometimes set in the Wild West, these are tales that contain extreme exaggeration and were never true.

Literary Response and Analysis Skills

<u>Formal and Informal Assessments</u>
Summative assessments are a formal way of assessing students' knowledge at the end of a unit of study. These types of assessments consist of formal tests and projects that "summarize" what students have learned during a course of study or at the conclusion of an instructional period in reading, such as at the end of a novel of focus. These assessments evaluate what a student has learned, and if he or she met the expectations of what was taught. They are often graded and used as scores in a teacher's grade book.

Informal assessments, or formative assessments, collect information that instructors can use to quickly evaluate students' progress and learning. As mentioned, informal assessments can be used after modeling or direct instruction to break students into intervention groups. Informal assessments can also be used as a pre-screening, prior to skill instruction, to see what students already know about the topic.

<u>Interpreting Results from These Assessments:</u>
Teachers can use formal tests as a way to form intervention groups before a new unit of study is introduced, or prior to another summative assessment, like standardized tests. Formal assessments allow teachers to identify which students require further instruction or re-teaching skills, especially before another formal assessment. The overall goal is for students to gain a full understanding of skills and to ensure skill mastery before the end of the grade level. Therefore, skills may need to be remediated and then reassessed. If skills are retaught and not reassessed, an instructor has no idea how a student has progressed.

<u>Planning Effective Instruction and Interventions</u>
Assessments (either summative or formative) are important to develop future lessons in the classroom. Teachers should constantly assess their students for understanding. A teacher should not move onto another topic without knowing if students understood the previous skill. Reading comprehension builds from prior experiences. Texts get more difficult and complex as the years go on. For example, if a

struggling student is passed on to the next grade level without any prior interventions in place, he or she may not have mastered certain skills. For this reason, ongoing assessments are important.

Using Informational, Descriptive, and Persuasive Materials

It is important for students to be exposed to a variety of texts, reading materials, and resources. To become well-rounded readers, teachers should provide students with expository texts in addition to the classroom textbooks. Key characteristics of informational and expository texts include informative facts about a specific topic. Since these are nonfiction texts, diagrams or other graphic aids may be used to assist in understanding the text. Other forms of informational text include news articles, research journals, educational magazines with informational text, and websites. These texts can be used in small groups or can be introduced in whole group instruction, and then further explored in small intervention groups.

Fact-based understanding and the use of textual evidence is imperative in expository and informational texts. Students should be able to compare and contrast two different texts and identify problems and solutions as well as cause and effect. Graphic organizers arranged chronologically can help students take notes when covering nonfiction texts. Students need to have the correct order of events in a nonfiction piece in order to identify the cause of an event, as well as the effect it had on problems and solutions. At times, students may need to compare and contrast two texts to identify the similarity of facts, the differences in reported facts, or note any bias from the author. Using knowledge of writing standards and instruction can aid students' understanding of informational text. When comprehending an informative text's objective, students should utilize their prior knowledge of the topic, prior writing assignments, and concluding sentences in the text. This is another example of how reading comprehension and writing go hand-in-hand in the learning process, and how writing and language become important to student comprehension.

Reading in the Content Areas

Although independent reading is important for students to cultivate a love of reading, reading in the content areas is another way to stimulate reading skills while also learning about other subjects at the same time. **Content areas** are main subject areas like Math, English, Social Studies, and Science. Reading in the content areas is the idea that reading is an integral part of each and every subject and not simply a practice all by itself. The **three-phase model of reading** is a set of steps that depicts the stages before, during, and after reading.

This model is used to identify reading strategies for content-area reading:

- **Pre-Reading**: In the pre-reading stage, students construct background information, make predictions, connect to personal life, and activate prior knowledge and experience. During this stage, activities that can take place include setting a purpose, developing vocabulary, studying of high-frequency words, and the use of graphic organizers.

- **During Reading**: In this stage, students return to the purpose of the text, find the main idea, identify details, find the organizing structure of the text, and draw conclusions. This stage allows students to speculate about the text, express their opinions, connect to other text, question and critically analyze the text, question the author, and interpret character behavior.

- **Post-Reading**: In the post-reading stage, students will summarize the text, learn to retell the information, connect to personal life, and discuss or interpret the motivation of the author. This stage includes making judgments, dealing with graphic organizers, illustrating or acting out a storyline, and connecting to the ideas used in other texts.

This model of reading is an important tool to use when teaching in the content areas because it goes beyond reading for pleasure and encourages students to think critically about whatever subject they may be reading about. In a Social Studies text, this model of reading will help students to draw upon their prior knowledge of Social Studies by discussing the event beforehand, actively read to find the purpose and details embedded within the text, and finally summarize the text and analyze the events that have just been learned through the reading phase.

Metacognitive Strategies

Metacognitive strategies ask the student to decode text passages. In part, they require the student to preview text, be able to recognize unfamiliar words, then use context clues to define them for greater understanding. In addition, meta-cognitive strategies in the classroom employ skills such as being able to decode imagery, being able to predict, and being able to summarize. If a student can define unfamiliar vocabulary, make sense of an author's use of imagery, preview text prior to reading predict outcomes during reading, and summarize the material, he or she is achieving effective reading comprehension. When approaching reading instruction, the teacher who encourages students to use phrases such as *I'm noticing*, *I'm thinking*, and *I'm wondering* is teaching a meta-cognitive type strategy.

Pre-Reading Strategies
Pre-reading strategies are important, yet often overlooked. Non-critical readers will often begin reading without taking the time to review factors that will help them understand the text. Skipping pre-reading strategies may result in a reader having to re-address a text passage more times than is necessary. Some pre-reading strategies include the following:

- Previewing the text for clues
- Skimming the text for content
- Scanning for unfamiliar words in context
- Formulating questions on sight
- Making predictions
- Recognizing needed prior knowledge

Before reading a text passage, a reader can enhance his or her ability to comprehend material by *previewing the text for clues*. This may mean making careful note of any titles, headings, graphics, notes, introductions, important summaries, and conclusions. It can involve a reader making physical notes regarding these elements or highlighting anything he or she thinks is important before reading. Often, a reader will be able to gain information just from these elements alone. Of course, close reading is required in order to fill in the details. A reader needs to be able to ask what he or she is reading about and what a passage is trying to say. The answers to these general questions can often be answered in previewing the text itself.

It's helpful to use pre-reading clues to determine the main idea and organization. First, any titles, sub-headings, chapter headings should be read, and the test taker should make note of the author's credentials if any are listed. It's important to deduce what these clues may indicate as it pertains to the focus of the text and how it's organized.

During pre-reading, readers should also take special note of how text features contribute to the central idea or thesis of the passage. Is there an index? Is there a glossary? What headings, footnotes, or other visuals are included and how do they relate to the details within the passage? Again, this is where any pre-reading notes come in handy, since a test taker should be able to relate supporting details to these textual features.

Next, a reader should *skim* the text for general ideas and content. This technique does not involve close reading; rather, it involves looking for important words within the passage itself. These words may have something to do with the author's theme. They may have to do with structure—for example, words such as *first, next, therefore*, and *last*. Skimming helps a reader understand the overall structure of a passage and, in turn, this helps him or her understand the author's theme or message.

From there, a reader should quickly *scan* the text for any unfamiliar words. When reading a print text, highlighting these words or making other marginal notation is helpful when going back to read text critically. A reader should look at the words surrounding any unfamiliar ones to see what contextual clues unfamiliar words carry. Being able to define unfamiliar terms through contextual meaning is a critical skill in reading comprehension.

A reader should also *formulate any questions* he or she might have before conducting close reading. Questions such as "What is the author trying to tell me?" or "Is the author trying to persuade my thinking?" are important to a reader's ability to engage critically with the text. Questions will focus a reader's attention on what is important in terms of idea and what is supporting detail.

Along with formulating questions, it is helpful to make predictions of what the answers to these questions and others will be. *Making predictions* involves using information from the text and personal experiences to make a thoughtful guess as to what will happen in the story and what outcomes can be expected.

Last, a reader should recognize that authors assume readers bring a *prior knowledge* set to the reading experience. Not all readers have the same experience, but authors seek to communicate with their readers. In turn, readers should strive to interact with the author of a particular passage by asking themselves what the passage demands they know during reading. This is also known as making a text-to-self connection. If a passage is informational in nature, a reader should ask "What do I know about this topic from other experiences I've had or other works I've read?" If a reader can relate to the content, he or she will better understand it.

All of the above pre-reading strategies will help the reader prepare for a closer reading experience. They will engage a reader in active interaction with the text by helping to focus the reader's full attention on the details that he or she will encounter during the next round or two of critical, closer reading.

Strategies During Reading

After pre-reading, a test taker can employ a variety of other reading strategies while conducting one or more closer readings. These strategies include the following:

- Clarifying during a close read
- Questioning during a close read
- Organizing the main ideas and supporting details
- Summarizing the text effectively

A reader needs to be able to *clarify* what he or she is reading. This strategy demands a reader think about how and what he or she is reading. This thinking should occur during and after the act of reading. For example, a reader may encounter one or more unfamiliar ideas during reading, then be asked to apply thoughts about those unfamiliar concepts after reading when answering test questions.

Questioning during a critical read is closely related to clarifying. A reader must be able to ask questions in general about what he or she is reading and questions regarding the author's supporting ideas. Questioning also involves a reader's ability to self-question. When closely reading a passage, it's not enough to simply try and understand the author. A reader must consider critical thinking questions to ensure he or she is comprehending intent. It's advisable, when conducting a close read, to write out margin notes and questions during the experience. These questions can be addressed later in the thinking process after reading and during the phase where a reader addresses the test questions. A reader who is successful in reading comprehension will iteratively question what he or she reads, search text for clarification, then answer any questions that arise.

A reader should *organize* main ideas and supporting details cognitively as he or she reads, as it will help the reader understand the larger structure at work. The use of quick annotations or marks to indicate what the main idea is and how the details function to support it can be helpful. Understanding the structure of a text passage is sometimes critical to answering questions about an author's approach, theme, messages, and supporting detail. This strategy is most effective when reading informational or nonfiction text. Texts that try to convince readers of a particular idea, that present a theory, or that try to explain difficult concepts are easier to understand when a reader can identify the overarching structure at work.

Post-Reading Strategies

After completing a text, a reader should be able to *summarize* the author's theme and supporting details in order to fully understand the passage. Being able to effectively restate the author's message, sub-themes, and pertinent, supporting ideas will help a reader gain an advantage when addressing standardized test questions.

A reader should also evaluate the strength of the predictions that were made in the pre-reading stage. Using textual evidence, predictions should be compared to the actual events in the story to see if the two were similar or not. Employing all of these strategies will lead to fuller, more insightful reading comprehension.

Author's Purpose

Expository texts typically share information about a given topic. *Persuasive texts* aim to convince readers to think or act a certain way, and *procedural texts* generally give step-by-step or "how-to" instructions in a given discipline. *Nonfiction narratives* tell a true story, perhaps to inspire, educate, bring awareness to a subject, or simply chronicle an important historical event. In order for students to become independent readers and draw their own conclusions about what they read, it is critical that they learn to discern the *author's purpose.*

One obvious approach to teaching children how to reveal an author's purpose is to simply ask children why they think the author wrote this information. These types of open-ended class discussions allow children to express their ideas, explore theories, and consider what others have to say on the subject. Educators can record various answers and then ask the children to return to the text as detectives, looking for clues that support each theory.

Another approach to uncovering the author's purpose is for students to take a closer look at the written structure of the text and the vocabulary usage. For example, is the text's structure written in chronological order, simply listing events as they occurred? Does the text open up with a problem that is then resolved? Is the author using cause/effect or compare/contrast vocabulary? Learning about the structure of the text gives great insight into the author's purpose.

When children develop reading fluency, they are able to read a text with minimal to no errors, with consistent speed, and with appropriate expression, and they learn to connect with what they are reading on a personal level. As children read through an informational text, educators may ask how the students are feeling. Did they begin feeling one way and end up feeling another by the end of the text? When children examine their own personal feelings with regard to what they have read, they will be in a better position to explore the author's purpose.

Once children have had several opportunities to explore the author's purpose using a variety of informational texts, prompting them to write their own informational texts will help them to develop and strengthen a better understanding about writing with a purpose. Perhaps they can write a procedural text that lists the steps in how to ride a bike, or they can write a persuasive paper to try to convince their teacher that extra free time during the school day stimulates learning.

Learning to identify an author's purpose connects children with their reading on a deeper level. Instead of believing everything they read, they will begin to understand that there are many reasons why authors write, and they will further understand that they possess the ability to draw their own conclusions and make their own decisions on any given topic.

Topic Versus the Main Idea

It is important to know the difference between the topic and the main idea of the passage. Even though these two are similar, they have some differences. A topic is the subject of the text. It can usually be described in a one- to two-word phrase. On the other hand, the main idea is more detailed. It provides the author's central point of the passage. It can be expressed through a complete sentence. It is often found in the beginning, middle, or end of a paragraph. In most nonfiction books, the first sentence of the passage usually states the main idea. Take a look at the passage below to review the topicversus the main idea.

> Cheetahs are one of the fastest mammals on land, reaching up to seventy miles an hour over short distances. Even though cheetahs can run as fast as seventy miles an hour, they usually only have to run half that speed to catch up with their choice of prey. Cheetahs cannot maintain a fast pace over long periods of time because they will overheat their bodies. After a chase, cheetahs need to rest for approximately thirty minutes prior to eating or returning to any other activity.

In the example above, the topic of the passage is Cheetahs because that is the subject of the text. The main idea of the text is "Cheetahs are one of the fastest mammals on the land but can only maintain a fast pace for shorter distances." While this covers the topic, it is more detailed. It refers to the text in its entirety. The passage provides more details called supporting details. These will be discussed in the next section.

Supporting Details

Supporting details help you understand the main idea. Supporting details answer questions like *who, what, where, when, why,* and *how.* Supporting details can include examples, facts, statistics, small stories, and visual details.

Persuasive and informative texts often use supporting details. In persuasive texts, authors try to make readers agree with their points of view. In persuasive texts, supporting details are often used as "selling points." If authors say something, they should support it with evidence. This helps to persuade readers. Informative texts use supporting details to inform readers. Take another look at the "Cheetahs" example from the page before to find examples of supporting details.

In the Cheetah example above, supporting details include:

- Cheetahs reach up to seventy miles per hour over short distances.
- Cheetahs usually only have to run half that speed to catch up with their prey.
- Cheetahs will overheat their bodies if they exert a high speed over longer distances.
- They need to rest for thirty minutes after a chase.

Look at the diagram below (applying the cheetah example) to help determine the hierarchy of topic, main idea, and supporting details.

Text Features and Organizational Patterns

Informational text is specifically designed to relate factual information, and although it is open to a reader's interpretation and application of the facts, the structure of the presentation is carefully designed to lead the reader to a particular conclusion or central idea. When reading informational text, it is important that readers are able to understand its organizational structure as the structure often directly relates to an author's intent to inform and/or persuade the reader.

The first step in identifying the text's structure is to determine the thesis or main idea. The thesis statement and organization of a work are closely intertwined. *A thesis statement* indicates the writer's purpose and may include the scope and direction of the text. It may be presented at the beginning of a text or at the end, and it may be explicit or implicit.

Once a reader has a grasp of the thesis or main idea of the text, he or she can better determine its organizational structure. Test takers are advised to read informational text passages more than once in order to comprehend the material fully. It is also helpful to examine any text features present in the text including the table of contents, index, glossary, headings, footnotes, and visuals. The analysis of these features and the information presented within them, can offer additional clues about the central idea and structure of a text. The following questions should be asked when considering structure:

- How does the author assemble the parts to make an effective whole argument?

- Is the passage linear in nature and if so, what is the timeline or thread of logic?

- What is the presented order of events, facts, or arguments? Are these effective in contributing to the author's thesis?

- How can the passage be divided into sections? How are they related to each other and to the main idea or thesis?

- What key terms are used to indicate the organization?

Next, test takers should skim the passage, noting the first line or two of each body paragraph—the *topic sentences*—and the conclusion. Key *transitional terms*, such as *on the other hand*, *also*, *because*, *however*, *therefore*, *most importantly*, and *first*, within the text can also signal organizational structure. Based on these clues, readers should then be able to identify what type of organizational structure is being used. The following organizational structures are most common:

- Problem/solution—organized by an analysis/overview of a problem, followed by potential solution(s)

- Cause/effect—organized by the effects resulting from a cause or the cause(s) of a particular effect

- Spatial order—organized by points that suggest location or direction—e.g., top to bottom, right to left, outside to inside

- Chronological/sequence order—organized by points presented to indicate a passage of time or through purposeful steps/stages

- Comparison/Contrast—organized by points that indicate similarities and/or differences between two things or concepts

- Order of importance—organized by priority of points, often most significant to least significant or vice versa

Text Structures

Writing can be classified under four passage types: narrative, expository, technical, and persuasive. Though these types are not mutually exclusive, one form tends to dominate the rest. By recognizing the *type* of passage you're reading, you gain insight into *how* you should read. If you're reading a narrative, you can assume the author intends to entertain, which means you may skim the text without losing meaning. A technical document might require a close read, because skimming the passage might cause the reader to miss salient details.

1. *Narrative* writing, at its core, is the art of storytelling. For a narrative to exist, certain elements must be present. It must have characters. While many characters are human, characters could be defined as anything that thinks, acts, and talks like a human. For example, many recent movies, such as *Lord of the Rings* and *The Chronicles of Narnia*, include animals, fantastical creatures, and even trees that behave like humans. It must have a plot or sequence of events. Typically, those events follow a standard plot diagram, but recent trends start *in medias res* or in the middle (near the climax). In this instance, foreshadowing and flashbacks often fill in plot details. Along with characters and a plot, there must also be conflict. Conflict is usually divided into two types: internal and external. Internal conflict indicates the character is in turmoil. Internal conflicts are presented through the character's thoughts. External conflicts are visible. Types of external conflict include a person versus nature, another person, and society.

2. *Expository* writing is detached and to the point, while other types of writing—persuasive, narrative, and descriptive—are lively. Since expository writing is designed to instruct or inform, it usually involves directions and steps written in second person ("you" voice) and lacks any persuasive or narrative elements. Sequence words such as *first*, *second*, and *third*, or *in the first place*, *secondly*, and *lastly* are often given to add fluency and cohesion. Common examples of expository writing include instructor's lessons, cookbook recipes, and repair manuals.

3. Due to its empirical nature, *technical* writing is filled with steps, charts, graphs, data, and statistics. The goal of technical writing is to advance understanding in a field through the scientific method. Experts such as teachers, doctors, or mechanics use words unique to the profession in which they operate. These words, which often incorporate acronyms, are called *jargon*. Technical writing is a type of expository writing but is not meant to be understood by the general public. Instead, technical writers assume readers have received a formal education in a particular field of study and need no explanation as to what the jargon means. Imagine a doctor trying to understand a diagnostic reading for a car or a mechanic trying to interpret lab results. Only professionals with proper training will fully comprehend the text.

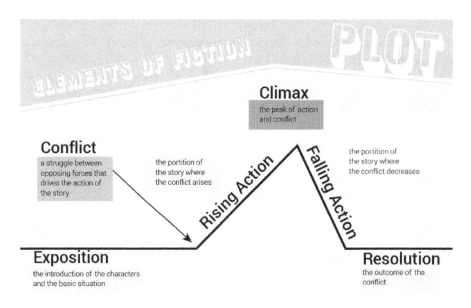

4. *Persuasive* writing is designed to change opinions and attitudes. The topic, stance, and arguments are found in the thesis, positioned near the end of the introduction. Later supporting paragraphs offer relevant quotations, paraphrases, and summaries from primary or secondary sources, which are then interpreted, analyzed, and evaluated. The goal of persuasive writers is not to stack quotes, but to develop original ideas by using sources as a starting point. Good persuasive writing makes powerful arguments with valid sources and thoughtful analysis. Poor persuasive writing is riddled with bias and logical fallacies. Sometimes, logical and illogical arguments are sandwiched together in the same piece. Therefore, readers should display skepticism when reading persuasive arguments.

Organization of a Text

There are five basic elements inherent in effective writing, and each will be discussed throughout the various subheadings of this section.

- *Main idea*: The driving message of the writing, clearly stated or implied

- *Clear organization*: The effective and purposeful arrangement of the content to support the main idea

- *Supporting details/evidence*: Content that gives appropriate depth and weight to the main idea of the story, argument, or information

- *Diction/tone*: The type of language, vocabulary, and word choice used to express the main idea, purposefully aligned to the audience and purpose

- *Adherence to conventions of English*: Correct spelling, grammar, punctuation, and sentence structure, allowing for clear communication of ideas

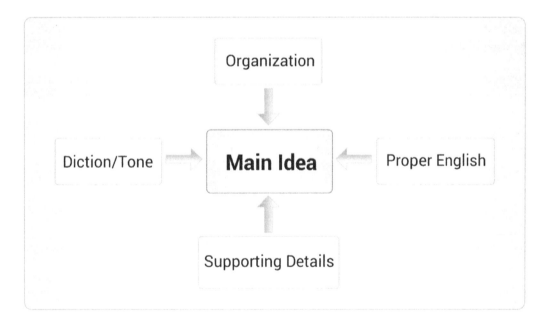

Digital Media

Using Technology Tools for Effective Communication

Different technological tools serve different functions. To function in the developing world, students need to learn and understand *digital literacy*—the knowledge, dexterity, and critical thinking skills involved in using technology to create, evaluate, and present information. The best techniques for instructing students on choosing and using technological tools involve educating them on the advantages and disadvantages of each, demonstrating how to use them, breaking down their different aspects, assigning students homework or projects in which they will utilize different technological resources, and instructing them on when it is appropriate to use each kind. The most common types of tools used for communication are as follows:

- Smartphones/apps
- Email
- Microsoft Office
- iMovie
- Skype
- Twitter
- Facebook
- Instagram
- Google Drive
- Various blogging websites
- Online bulletin boards
- Wikis

A good way to introduce students to varying technological tools is by using them in the classroom. It would be helpful to teach students how to use a PowerPoint presentation, for example, by giving a PowerPoint presentation. If a student asks a question to which the teacher does not know the answer, they can discover the answer together by using a reliable source on the Internet, projecting the process on the board, so that they can see exactly how it's done. Students can also receive homework and updates on school and classroom events through a personal blog or class bulletin board the teacher has designed so that they may become familiar with using online communication. Students can also be assigned to use personal blogs to practice and improve their writing skills.

The most effective method for learning new skills is a hands-on approach. Students can be educated on the pros and cons of each technological tool, but the best way for them to learn is to allow them to find out for themselves by assigning projects and asking them to give the reasoning behind choosing a specific tool. For example, they may be asked to do a project on some aspect of the Revolutionary War by choosing a media format. Ideas may include the following:

- Doing a presentation

- Filming and editing a video re-enactment of a great battle

- Writing a script in Microsoft Word or in a Google doc and having classmates act it out

- Creating Facebook statuses from the viewpoints of the forefathers in modern colloquial language

- Having a "Twitter war" between the British and the Colonials

- Asking various people to participate in a collaborative Wiki or Google Doc in which many people give their versions of aspects of the Revolutionary War

- Writing a blog narrating life as a soldier

- Posting photos of the signing of the Declaration of Independence

Students can then give their presentations to the classroom so that students can learn about the topic through different presentation styles.

Another way to engage students in using technology is to have them communicate with each other through the various methods of communication—e.g., starting a class Google Doc, creating a classroom Facebook group, or using a discussion board. This is also an excellent opportunity to encourage students to use Standard English through all methods of communication to enhance their writing skills and instill a sense of professionalism, which they will need throughout their lives.

For example, requiring that all students use complete sentences, proper spelling, and grammar through Facebook, Twitter, or blogs associated with homework or projects will encourage them to do so in their daily lives as well. Another example is requiring that students select tweets from their favorite celebrities or politicians, analyze their meaning and purpose, correct their grammar and spelling, and re-tweet them in the correct way. There are countless ways in which technology can be used in the classroom to enhance students' understanding of digital communication; all it requires is a little creativity.

Evaluating Technology-Based Strategies
It is hard to find a technological tool that will not be useful for students to explore. The more a student engages with the numerous different types of technology, the more digitally literate that student will become. Each type is effective and brings value to the table in its own way. When evaluating the effectiveness of a specific technology-based strategy, it's important to consider how this method is enhancing the student's digital literacy, as well as their critical thinking and communication skills. It is also necessary to evaluate the technology itself by asking relevant questions:

- Is it appropriate for the average age of the students in the classroom?
- Is it user friendly?
- Does it work consistently?
- Are there multiple ways to get help on learning how to use it?
- Are there trouble-shooting options?
- Does it have good reviews?
- Is it relevant to the content of the curriculum?
- Does it support and align to the learning objective?
- Is it more distracting than it is useful?
- Is it a tool that is/will be used often in the real world?
- Can it be used for more than one project or assignment?

One very effective teaching strategy is *collaborative learning*, in which two or more students work together to develop a project, work through an idea, or solve a problem. This method allows for students to play off each other's strengths and different experiences and learn how to communicate with their classmates to achieve goals. Technology can be used for collaborative learning in Google Drive, Skype, Google Hangouts, Neapod, Padlet, and Periscope, in creating PowerPoint presentations together, or by conducting surveys with websites like Survey Monkey.

Another effective teaching method is *discussion*, in which students are given a topic or create a topic themselves and then use technology to engage in discourse. This can be done via discussion boards, such as ProBoards or Boardhost, or done live through programs such as Skype or Hangouts. Discussion strategies are extremely effective for enhancing communication skills and digital literacy.

A third method is *active learning*, in which the student engages in activities such as reading, writing, or teaching the subject to another student. Blogging is a great way to encourage active learning as it provides a medium through which students can reflect on what they've learned and respond to comments posted by the teacher or other students. Most of the suggestions made in the previous section—making presentations, creating video re-enactments, writing scripts, having mock Twitter or Facebook comment wars—are all forms of active learning. These types of activities solidify events, ideas, and skills in a student's mind in a way that memorization or flashcards do not as they utilize many different types of thinking and interaction.

One method that a teacher may employ depending on the class and circumstances is *distance learning*. Distance learning is any type of teaching method in which the student and teacher are not in the same place simultaneously. Many professors utilize distance learning through different kinds of technologies, including a live virtual lecture, computer simulations, interactive discussions, and virtual/audio learning environments. These strategies have their advantages in that one teacher can teach a large number of students and multiple locations, and students can communicate with fellow classmates across the globe.

Auditory learning is a strategy in which a student learns through listening. This typically happens via recorded lectures that can be downloaded as podcasts onto a classroom website, discussion board, or some other audio-simulated learning environment. *Visual learning* is learning through watching, in which ideas and concepts are illustrated through images, videos, or by observing a teacher complete a task, explain a concept, or solve a problem. This can be achieved through recorded videos, cartoons, virtual lectures, or by sitting in the classroom. Additionally, *kinesthetic learning* is active learning through physical interaction with an object or actively solving a problem, as opposed to passively listening or watching.

Every student has a different learning style which is unique to them—some learn better through listening while others learn better through doing. The best teaching methods employ all different learning strategies so that all the senses are engaged and every student has a chance at learning material based on their individual learning needs. Technology offers educators the tools do that.

Using Evidence to Support Predictions, Opinions, and Conclusions

Text evidence is the information readers find in a text or passage that supports the main idea or point(s) in a story. In turn, text evidence can help readers draw conclusions about the text or passage. The information should be taken directly from the text or passage and placed in quotation marks. Text evidence provides readers with information to support ideas about the text so that they do not rely simply on their own thoughts. Details should be precise, descriptive, and factual. Statistics are a great piece of text evidence because they provide readers with exact numbers and not just a generalization. For example, instead of saying "Asia has a larger population than Europe," authors could provide detailed information such as, "In Asia there are over 4 billion people, whereas in Europe there are a little over 750 million." More definitive information provides better evidence to readers to help support their conclusions about texts or passages.

Practice Questions

1. What contributes the most to schema development?
    a. Reading comprehension
    b. Structural analysis
    c. Written language
    d. Background knowledge

2. Which of the following is NOT an essential component of effective fluency instruction?
    a. Spelling
    b. Feedback
    c. Guidance
    d. Practice

3. The Directed-Reading Think-Aloud (DRTA) method helps students to do what?
    a. Build prior knowledge by exploring audiovisual resources before a reading
    b. Predict what will occur in a text and search the text to verify the predictions
    c. Identify, define, and review unfamiliar terms
    d. Understand the format of multiple types and genres of text

4. A teacher assigns a writing prompt in order to assess her students' reading skills. Which of the following can be said about this form of reading assessment?
    a. It is the most beneficial way to assess reading comprehension
    b. It is invalid because a student's ability to read and write are unrelated
    c. It is erroneous since the strength of a student's reading and writing vocabulary may differ
    d. It is the worst way to assess reading comprehension

5. When does scaffolded reading occur?
    a. A student hears a recording of herself reading a text in order to set personal reading goals.
    b. A student receives assistance and feedback on strategies to utilize while reading from someone else.
    c. A student is given extra time to find the answers to predetermined questions.
    d. A student is pulled out of a class to receive services elsewhere.

6. What are the three interconnected indicators of reading fluency?
    a. Phonetics, word morphology, and listening comprehension
    b. Accuracy, rate, and prosody
    c. Syntax, semantics, and vocabulary
    d. Word exposure, phonetics, and decodable skills

7. Which of the following about effective independent reading is NOT true?
    a. Students should read texts that are below their reading levels during independent reading.
    b. Students need to first demonstrate fluency before reading independently.
    c. Students who don't yet display automaticity should whisper to themselves when reading aloud.
    d. Students who demonstrate automaticity in decoding should be held accountable during independent reading.

8. Timed oral reading can be used to assess which of the following?
    a. Phonics
    b. Listening comprehension
    c. Reading rate
    d. Background knowledge

9. Syntax is best described as what?
    a. The arrangement of words into sentences
    b. The study of language meaning
    c. The study of grammar and language structure
    d. The proper formatting of a written text

10. What do informal reading assessments allow that standardized reading assessments do NOT allow?
    a. The application of grade-level norms towards a student's reading proficiency
    b. The personalization of reading assessments in order to differentiate instruction based on the need(s) of individual students
    c. The avoidance of partialities in the interpretation of reading assessments
    d. The comparison of an individual's reading performance to that of other students in the class

11. When building a class library, a teacher should be cognizant of the importance of what?
    a. Providing fiction that contains concepts relating to the background knowledge of all students in the class.
    b. Utilizing only nonfictional text that correlates to state and national standards in order to reinforce academic concept knowledge.
    c. Utilizing a single genre of text in order to reduce confusion of written structures.
    d. Including a wide range of fiction and nonfiction texts at multiple reading levels.

12. Samantha is in second grade and struggles with fluency. Which of the following strategies is likely to be most effective in improving Samantha's reading fluency?
    a. The teacher prompts Samantha when she pauses upon coming across an unknown word when reading aloud.
    b. The teacher records Samantha as she reads aloud.
    c. The teacher reads a passage out loud several times to Samantha and then has Samantha read the same passage.
    d. The teacher uses read-alouds and verbalizes contextual strategies that can be used to identify unfamiliar words.

13. Reading fluency is best described as the ability to do what?
    a. Read smoothly and accurately
    b. Comprehend what is read
    c. Demonstrate phonetic awareness
    d. Properly pronounce a list of words

14. Poems are often an effective device when teaching what skill?
    a. Fluency
    b. Spelling
    c. Writing
    d. Word decoding

15. A teacher needs to assess students' accuracy in reading grade-appropriate, high frequency, and irregular sight words. Which of the following strategies would be most appropriate for this purpose?

    a. The teacher gives students a list of words to study for a spelling test that will be administered the following week.

    b. The teacher allows each student to bring their favorite book from home and has each student read their selected text aloud independently.

    c. The teacher administers the Stanford Structural Analysis assessment to determine students' rote memory and application of morphemes contained within the words.

    d. The teacher records how many words each student reads correctly when reading aloud a list of a teacher-selected, grade-appropriate words.

16 What type of text(s) should be included when teaching reading comprehension in the classroom?

    a. Expository/informational

    b. Nonfiction and fiction

    c. Only nonfiction

    d. Basal readers

17. What is a summative assessment?

    a. A formal assessment that is given at the end of a unit of study

    b. An informal assessment that is given at the end of a unit of study

    c. An assessment that is given daily and is usually only a few questions in length, based on the day's objective

    d. An assessment given at the end of the week that is usually based on observation

18. How are typographic features useful when teaching reading comprehension?

    a. Typographic features are graphics used to illustrate the story and help students visualize the text.

    b. Typographic features give the answers in boldfaced print.

    c. Typographic features are not helpful when teaching reading comprehension and should not be used.

    d. Typographic features are print in boldface, italics, and subheadings, used to display changes in topics or to highlight important vocabulary or content.

19. What do English Language Learners need to identify prior to comprehending text?

    a. Vocabulary

    b. Figurative language

    c. Author's purpose

    d. Setting

20. What kind of assessment is most beneficial for students with special needs?

    a. Frequent and ongoing

    b. Weekly

    c. Monthly

    d. Summative assessments only at the end of a unit of study

21. Which is NOT a reason that independent reading is important for developing reading comprehension?
    a. To develop a lifelong love of reading
    b. To encourage students to read a genre they enjoy
    c. So that students can read at their own pace
    d. To visit the reading corner, which is an area of the classroom that is restful and enjoyable

22. Why are purposeful read alouds by a teacher important to enhance reading comprehension?
    a. They encourage students to unwind from a long day and reading lesson.
    b. They encourage students to listen for emphasis and voice.
    c. They encourage students to compare the author's purpose versus the teacher's objective.
    d. They encourage students to work on important work from earlier in the day while listening to a story.

23. Which of the following is the definition of *syntax*?
    a. The meaning of words
    b. The order of words in a sentence
    c. The grouping of large complex words
    d. Highlighted, or boldfaced words

24. What is "text evidence" when referring to answering a comprehension question?
    a. Taking phrases directly from the text itself to answer a question
    b. Using a variety of resources to find the answer
    c. Using technology and websites to locate an answer
    d. Paraphrasing and using a student's own words to answer the question

25. What allows readers to effectively translate print into recognizable speech?
    a. Fluency
    b. Spelling
    c. Phonics
    d. Word decoding

26. Which of the following is the MOST important reason why group-based discussions in the classroom enhance reading comprehension?
    a. They promote student discussions without the teacher present.
    b. They promote student discussions with a friend.
    c. They promote student discussions so that those who didn't understand the text can get answers from another student.
    d. They give all students a voice and allow them to share their answer, rather than one student sharing an answer with the class

27. Which of the following skills is NOT useful when initially helping students understand and comprehend a piece of text?
    a. Graphic organizers
    b. Note-taking
    c. Small intervention groups
    d. Extension projects and papers

28. Why are intervention groups important to advanced learners?
    a. They are not useful, as they do not need intervention in a particular skill
    b. They can be used to teach struggling students
    c. They can be given more advanced and complex work
    d. They can be given tasks to do in the classroom while others are meeting for intervention

29. Which of the following can be useful when working with intervention groups of struggling readers?
    a. Having the teacher read aloud a text to the students while they take notes
    b. Having students read the text silently
    c. Giving independent work and explaining the directions in detail before they take it back to their seat
    d. Providing games for them to play while the teacher observes

30. What should be taught and mastered first when teaching reading comprehension?
    a. Theme
    b. Word analysis and fluency
    c. Text evidence
    d. Writing

31. What is the method called that teachers use before and after reading to improve critical thinking and comprehension?
    a. Self-monitoring comprehension
    b. KWL charts
    c. Metacognitive skills
    d. Directed reading-thinking activities

32. When a student looks back at a previous reading section for information, he or she is using which of the following?
    a. Self-monitoring comprehension
    b. KWL charts
    c. Metacognitive skills
    d. Directed reading-thinking activities

33. Which choice of skills is NOT part of Bloom's Taxonomy?
    a. Remembering and understanding
    b. Applying and analyzing
    c. Listening and speaking
    d. Evaluating and creating

34. What is the spelling stage of a student who looks at a word and is able to tell the teacher that the letters spell C-A-T, but the who cannot actually say the word?
    a. Alphabetic Spelling
    b. Within Word Pattern Spelling
    c. Derivational Relations Spelling
    d. Emergent Spelling

35. Predicting, Summarizing, Questioning, and Clarifying are steps of what?
    a. Reciprocal teaching
    b. Comprehensive teaching
    c. Activation teaching
    d. Summative teaching

36. When a student asks, "What do I know?", "What do I want to know?", and "What have I learned?" and records the answers in a table, he or she is using which of the following?
    a. Self-monitoring comprehension
    b. KWL charts
    c. Metacognitive skills
    d. Directed reading-thinking activities

37. What technique might an author use to let the reader know that the main character was in a car crash as a child?
    a. Point of view
    b. Characterization
    c. Figurative language
    d. Flashback

38. A graphic organizer is a method of achieving what?
    a. Integrating knowledge and ideas
    b. Generating questions
    c. Determining point of view
    d. Determining the author's purpose

39. A student is trying to decide if a character is telling the truth about having stolen candy. After the student reads that the character is playing with an empty candy wrapper in her pocket, the student decides the character is guilty. This is an example of what?
    a. Flashback
    b. Making inferences
    c. Style
    d. Figurative language

40. What is the method of categorizing text by its structure and literary elements called?
    a. Fiction
    b. Nonfiction
    c. Genre
    d. Plot

41. A reader is distracted from following a story because he's having trouble understanding why a character has decided to cut school, so the reader jumps to the next page to find out where the character is headed. This is an example of what?
    a. Self-monitoring comprehension
    b. KWL charts
    c. Metacognitive skills
    d. Directed reading-thinking activities

42. Phonemic Awareness, Phonics, Fluency, Vocabulary, and Comprehension are the five basic elements of what?

    a. Bloom's Taxonomy

    b. Spelling instruction

    c. Reading education

    d. Genre

Answer Explanations

1. D: A schema is a framework or structure that stores and retrieves multiple, interrelated learning elements as a single packet of knowledge. Children who have greater exposure to life events have greater schemas. Thus, students who bring extensive background knowledge to the classroom are likely to experience easier automation when reading. In this way, background knowledge and reading comprehension are directly related. Likewise, students who have greater background knowledge are able to learn a greater number of new concepts at a faster rate.

2. A: Practice is an essential component of effective fluency instruction. When teachers provide daily opportunities for students to learn words and utilize word-analysis skills, accuracy and rate will likely increase. Oral reading accompanied by guidance and feedback from teachers, peers, or parents has a significant positive impact on fluency. In order to be beneficial, such feedback needs to target specific areas in which students need improvement, as well as strategies that students can use in order to improve their areas of need. Such feedback increases students' awareness so that they can independently make needed modifications to improve fluency.

3. B: DRTA, or Directed Reading-Thinking Activity, incorporates both read-alouds and think-alouds. During a DRTA, students make predictions about what they will read in order to set a purpose for reading, give cognitive focus, and activate prior knowledge. Students use reading comprehension in order to verify their predictions.

4. C: There are five types of vocabulary: listening, speaking, written, sight, and meaning. Most often, listening vocabulary contains the greatest number of words. This is usually followed by speaking vocabulary, sight reading vocabulary, meaning vocabulary, and written vocabulary. Formal written language usually utilizes a richer vocabulary than everyday oral language. Thus, students show differing strengths in reading vocabulary and writing vocabulary. Likewise, a student's reading ability will most likely differ when assessed via a reading assessment versus a writing sample.

5. B: Scaffolded opportunities occur when a teacher helps students by giving them support, offering immediate feedback, and suggesting strategies. In order to be beneficial, such feedback needs to help students identify areas that need improvement. Much like oral reading feedback, this advice increases students' awareness so they can independently make needed modifications in order to improve fluency.

Scaffolding is lessened as the student becomes a more independent reader. Struggling readers, students with reading difficulties or disabilities, and students with special needs especially benefit from direct instruction and feedback that teaches decoding and analysis of unknown words, automaticity in key sight words, and correct expression and phrasing.

6. B: Key indicators of reading fluency include accuracy, rate, and prosody. Phonetics and decodable skills aid fluency. Syntax, semantics, word morphology, listening comprehension, and word exposure aid vocabulary development.

7. A: Once students become fluent readers, independent reading can begin. Students who don't yet display automaticity may need to read out loud or whisper to themselves during independent reading time. Independent silent reading accompanied by comprehension accountability is an appropriate strategy for students who demonstrate automaticity in their decoding skills. Also, each student should be provided with a text that matches his or her reading level.

8. C: The most common measurement of reading rate includes the oral contextual timed readings of students. During a timed reading, the number of errors made within a given amount of time is recorded. This data can be used to identify if a student's rate is improving and if the rate falls within the recommended fluency rates for their grade level.

9. A: Syntax refers to the arrangement of words and phrases to form well-developed sentences and paragraphs. Semantics has to do with language meaning. Grammar is a composite of all systems and structures utilized within a language and includes syntax, word morphology, semantics, and phonology. Cohesion and coherence of oral and written language are promoted through a full understanding of syntax, semantics, and grammar.

10. B: Informal reading assessments allow teachers to create differentiated assessments that target reading skills of individual students. In this way, teachers can gain insight into a student's reading strengths and weaknesses. Informal assessments can help teachers decide what content and strategies need to be targeted. However, standardized reading assessments provide all students with the same structure to assess multiple skills at one time. Standardized reading assessments cannot be individualized. Such assessments are best used for gaining an overview of student reading abilities.

11. D: Students within a single classroom come with various background knowledge, interests, and needs. Thus, it's unrealistic to find texts that apply to all. Students benefit when a wide range of fiction and nonfiction texts are available in a variety of genres, promoting differentiated instruction.

12. D: This answer alludes to both read-alouds and think-alouds. Modeling of fluency can be done through read-alouds. Proper pace, phrasing, and expression of text can be modeled when teachers read aloud to their students. During think-alouds, teachers verbalize their thought processes when orally reading a selection. The teacher's explanations may describe strategies they use as they read to monitor their comprehension. In this way, teachers explicitly model the metacognition processes that good readers use to construct meaning from a text.

13. A: Reading fluency is the ability to accurately read at a socially acceptable pace and with proper expression. Phonetic awareness leads to the proper pronunciation of words and fluency. Once students are able to read fluently, concentration is no longer dedicated toward the process of reading. Instead, students can concentrate on the meaning of a text. Thus, in the developmental process of reading, comprehension follows fluency.

14. A: Poems are an effective method for teaching fluency, since rhythmic sounds and rhyming words build a child's understanding of phonemic awareness.

15. D: Accuracy is measured via the percentage of words that are read correctly with in a given text. Word-reading accuracy is often measured by counting the number of errors that occur per 100 words of oral reading. This information is used to select the appropriate level of text for an individual.

16. B: Nonfiction and fiction texts should both be used. This could encompass the Choices *A*, *C*, and *D*, which include expository, informational, nonfiction, and use of the school's basal reader, but should not be limited to just one of these. Utilizing many different types of text and genres when teaching reading comprehension is key to success.

17. A: Summative assessments are formal assessments that are given at the end of a unit of study. These assessments are usually longer in length. They are not completed daily. These summative assessments shouldn't be confused with informal assessments, which are used more frequently to determine mastery of the day's objective. However, summative assessments may be used to determine students' mastery, in order to form intervention groups thereafter.

18. D: Typographic features are important when teaching reading comprehension as the boldfaced, highlighted, or italics notify a student when a new vocabulary word or idea is present. Subtitles and headings can also alert a student to a change in topic or idea. These features are also important when answering questions, as a student may be able to easily find the answer with these typographic features present.

19. A: English Language Learners should master vocabulary and word usages in order to fully comprehend text. Figurative language, an author's purpose, and settings are more complex areas and are difficult for English Language Learners. These areas can be addressed once ELL students understand the meaning of words. In order to master comprehension skills, vocabulary and the English language need to be mastered first, but comprehension can still be difficult. Figurative language is culture-based, and inferences may be difficult for those with a different cultural background.

20. A: Assessments should always be frequent and ongoing for all students, but especially for those with special needs. These assessments may be informal, but given daily after direct instruction and modeling. Summative assessments are important, but this should not be the first and only assessment during a unit of study, as these types of assessments are given at the end of a unit of study. Weekly and monthly assessments are not frequent enough for instructors to identify struggling areas and for successful remediation and intervention.

21. D: Although the reading corner should be a restful and enjoyable place to encourage students to read independently, it does not enhance reading comprehension directly. Choices A, B, and C all encourage enhancement of reading comprehension. Giving students a chance to read independently allows them to choose books they enjoy, read at their own pace, and develop a lifelong enjoyment of reading.

22. B: Purposeful teacher read alouds allow students to listen to a story for voice emphasis and tone. This will help students when they are reading independently as well. Although students may find this time restful or a chance to catch up on old work, neither is the main purpose. Students may use this time to take notes on the reading, but students should only be listening to the story being read and not doing other work.

23. B: Syntax is the order of words in a sentence. The order of words in a sentence is important to meaning, but Choice A is not the direct definition of syntax. Choice C is incorrect because syntax does not mean grouping of complex words. Choice D is incorrect because highlighted and boldfaced words refer to typographic features in a text, not to syntax.

24. A: "Text evidence" refers to taking phrases and sentences directly from the text and writing them in the answer. Students are not asked to paraphrase, nor use any other resources to address the answer. Therefore, Choices B, C, and D are incorrect.

25. C: Phonics allows readers to effectively translate print into recognizable speech. It essentially enables young readers to translate printed words into recognizable speech. If children lack proficiency in phonics, their ability to read fluently and to increase vocabulary will be limited.

26. D: Text-based discussions, like think-pair-share, encourage all students to speak rather than having just one student share an answer. Each student is given time to collaborate with another student and share their thoughts. It is not intended for one student to give another student the answers, which is why Choice *C* is incorrect. Although Choices *A* and *B* might be correct, they are not the MOST important reason that text-based discussions are useful in the classroom.

27. D: Extension projects and papers should be used to challenge advanced learners, not learners developing comprehension skills. Graphic organizers, taking notes, and small intervention groups can aid reading comprehension. Graphic organizers and taking notes are great ways for a student to outline key parts of the text. Small intervention groups set up by the instructor can then focus on individual needs.

28. C: Advanced students can benefit from intervention groups by allowing the students to be challenged with more complex assignments. These assignments can be worked on independently and can include more difficult questions or higher level vocabulary. Even short projects may be beneficial for these advanced students to work on throughout the week.

29. A: Small intervention groups can benefit from a teacher reading a text or small book aloud while students listen and take notes. This helps struggling students to focus on reading comprehension rather than having to decode words. Intervention time is not meant for a teacher to give independent work nor to just provide observation without support.

30. B: Word analysis and fluency should be mastered before teaching theme, text evidence, and writing. For English Language Learners and struggling readers, word analysis and fluency are often difficult barriers, which is why comprehension skills are not initially mastered. Theme is often a complex and inferential skill, which is developed later on. Text evidence is pulling answers to comprehension questions directly from a text and cannot be accomplished until readers can fluently read and understand the text. Writing skills generally come after comprehension skills are underway.

31. D: Teachers use directed reading-thinking activities before and after reading to improve critical thinking and reading comprehension. Metacognitive skills are when learners think about their thinking. Self-monitoring is when children are asked to think as they read and ask themselves if what they have just read makes sense. KWL charts help guide students to identify what they already know about a given topic.

32. C: Asking oneself a comprehension question is a metacognition skill. Readers with metacognitive skills have learned to think about thinking. It gives students control over their learning while they read. KWL charts help students to identify what they already know about a given topic.

33. C: Listening and speaking are not part of Bloom's Taxonomy. The six parts are remembering, understanding, applying, analyzing, evaluating, and creating.

34. D: During the Emergent Spelling stage, children can identify letters but not the corresponding sounds. The other choices are all fictitious.

35. A: Reciprocal teaching involves predicting, summarizing, questioning, and clarifying. The other choices are all fictitious.

36. B: KWL charts are an effective method of activating prior knowledge and taking advantage of students' curiosity. Students can create a KWL (*Know/Want to know/Learned*) chart to prepare for any unit of instruction and to generate questions about a topic.

37. D: Flashback is a technique used to give more background information in a story. None of the other concepts are directly related to going back in time.

38. A: Graphic organizers are a method of integrating knowledge and ideas. A graphic organizer can be one of many different visual tools for connecting concepts to help students understand information.

39. B: Making inferences is a method of deriving meaning in writing that is intended by the author but not explicitly stated. A flashback is a scene set earlier than the main story. Style is a general term for the way something is done. Figurative language is text that is not to be taken literally.

40. C: Genre is a means of categorizing text by its structure and literary elements. Fiction and nonfiction are both genre categories. Plot is the sequence of events that make a story happen.

41. A: Scanning future portions of the text for information that helps resolve a question is an example of self-monitoring. Self-monitoring takes advantage students' natural ability to recognize when they understand the reading and when they do not. KWL charts are used to help guide students to identify what they already know about a given topic. Metacognitive skills are when learners think about their thinking. Directed reading-thinking activities are done before and after reading to improve critical thinking and reading comprehension skills.

42. C: The five basic components of reading education are phonemic awareness, phonics, fluency, vocabulary, and comprehension.

Writing in Support of Reading

Interdependence of Reading and Writing Development

Interdependence of Reading and Writing Development

The goal of sight word instruction is to help students readily recognize regular and irregular high-frequency words in order to aid reading fluency and comprehension. Several factors affect the sequence of instruction for specific sight words. For example, before a child is exposed to sight words, he or she needs to be able to fluently recognize and say the sound of all uppercase and lowercase letters. Also, students need to be able to accurately decode target words before they recognize sight words. When irregular words are introduced, attention should be drawn to both the phonetically regular and the phonetically irregular portions of the words.

Before sight word instruction can begin, teachers need to identify high-frequency words that do and do not follow normal spelling conventions, but are used often. Teachers may choose to select words that are used often within their students' reading materials, words that students have an interest in learning, or content-specific words. Alternatively, grade-level standardized sight word lists, such as the Dolch word lists, can be referenced.

Repetition and exposure through guided and independent practice are essential in student retention of sight words. Each lesson should introduce only three to five new sight words and also review words from previous lessons. Visually similar words should not be introduced in proximity to one another.

Sample activities through which sight words can be taught are listed below.

1. Students can practice reading decodable texts and word lists.

2. Teachers should read text that contains the sight words that a class is currently learning. As a teacher reads aloud, they should pause, point to, and correctly pronounce the words. Instead of pointing to the words, teachers can underline or highlight the words as they appear in sentences that are read.

3. Flashcards can be used to practice sight word recognition.

4. Games are fun and motivating avenues through which sight words can be practiced. Examples of games that can be used to practice sight words include Bingo, Go Fish, and Memory.

5. As students learn new sight words, they can write them in a sight word "dictionary." Students should be asked to write a sentence using each sight word included within the dictionary.

The spelling of high-frequency words should be taught after students have been exposed to the words, can readily recognize the words, and can read the words. The following multisensory strategies can be used to help students master the spelling of high-frequency sight words:

1. Spell Reading: Spell reading begins when a student says the high-frequency word. Then, the student spells out the letters in the word. Lastly, the student reads the word again. Spell reading helps commit the word to a student's memory when done in repetition.

2. Air Writing: When air writing, a student uses their finger to write the letters of a word in the air.

3. Arm Tapping: During arm tapping, a student says the word, spells the word's letters on their arm, and then reads the word again.

4. Table Writing: Students write the word on the table. A substrate, where the word is written in sand or shaving cream, can be added to the table. See examples of substrates below:

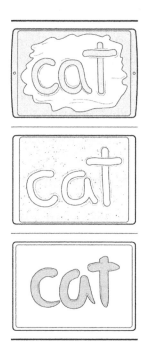

5. Letter Magnet Spelling: Arranging letter magnets on a metal surface, such as a cookie sheet, is a fun way for students to learn how to spell sight words. Because this strategy is seen as a game to the student, letter magnet spelling increases student motivation to write words.

6. Material Writing: Students can use clay, play dough, Wikki sticks, or other materials to form letters that are used to spell the words.

Writing as a Developmental Process

Almost all coherent written works contain three primary parts: a beginning, middle, and end. The organizational arrangements differ widely across distinct writing modes. Persuasive and expository texts utilize an introduction, body, and conclusion whereas narrative works use an orientation, series of events/conflict, and a resolution.

Every element within a written piece relates back to the main idea, and the beginning of a persuasive or expository text generally conveys the main idea or the purpose. For a narrative piece, the beginning is the section that acquaints the reader with the characters and setting, directing them to the purpose of the writing. The main idea in narrative may be implied or addressed at the end of the piece.

Depending on the primary purpose, the arrangement of the middle will adhere to one of the basic organizational structures described in the information texts and rhetoric section. They are cause and effect, problem and solution, compare and contrast, description/spatial, sequence, and order of importance.

The ending of a text is the metaphorical wrap-up of the writing. A solid ending is crucial for effective writing as it ties together loose ends, resolves the action, highlights the main points, or repeats the central idea. A **conclusion** ensures that readers come away from a text understanding the author's main idea. The table below highlights the important characteristics of each part of a piece of writing.

Structure	Argumentative/Informative	Narrative
Beginning	Introduction Purpose, main idea	Orientation Introduces characters, setting, necessary background
Middle	Body Supporting details, reasons, and evidence	Events/Conflict Story's events that revolve around a central conflict
End	Conclusion Highlights main points, summarizes and paraphrases ideas, reiterates the main idea	Resolution The solving of the central conflict

Spelling as a Developmental Process

Decoding and encoding are reciprocal phonological skills, meaning that the steps to each are opposite of one another.

Decoding is the application of letter-sound correspondences, letter patterns, and other phonics relationships that help students read and correctly pronounce words. Decoding helps students to recognize and read words quickly, increasing reading fluency and comprehension. The order of the steps that occur during the decoding process are as follows:

1. The student identifies a written letter or letter combination.

2. The student makes correlations between the sound of the letter or sounds of the letter combination.

3. The student understands how the letters or letter combinations fit together.

4. The student verbally blends the letter and letter combinations together to form a word.

Encoding is the spelling of words. In order to properly spell words, students must be familiar with letter/sound correspondences. Students must be able to put together phonemes, digraphs or blends, morphological units, consonant/vowel patterns, etc. The steps of encoding are identified below:

1. The student understands that letters and sounds make up words.

2. The student segments the sound parts of a word.

3. The student identifies the letter or letter combinations that correspond to each sound part.

4. The student then writes the letters and letter combinations in order to create the word.

Because the stages of decoding and spelling are essentially opposite of one another, they are reciprocal skills. Thus, phonics knowledge supports the development of reading and spelling. Likewise, the development of spelling knowledge reinforces phonics and decoding knowledge. In fact, the foundation of all good spelling programs is their alignment to reading instruction and a student's reading level.

Because of the reciprocal relationship between decoding and encoding, the development of phonics, vocabulary, and spelling are interrelated. The instruction of phonics begins with simple syllable patterns. Phonics instruction then progresses toward more difficult syllable patterns, more complex phonics patterns, the sounds of morphemes, and strategies for decoding multisyllabic words. Through this process, new vocabulary is developed. Sight word instruction should not begin until students are able to decode target words with automaticity and accuracy. Spelling is the last instructional component to be introduced.

Spelling development occurs in stages. In order, these stages are the pre-phonetic stage, the semiphonetic stage, the phonetic stage, the transitional stage, and the conventional stage. Each stage is explained below. Ways in which phonics and vocabulary development fit into the spelling stages are discussed. Instructional strategies for each phase of spelling are suggested.

Spelling development begins with the **pre-phonetic stage.** This stage is marked by an incomplete understanding of the alphabetic principle. Student understanding of letter-sound correspondences is limited. During the pre-phonetic stage, students participate in precommunicative writing. **Precommunicative writing** appears to be a jumble of letter-like forms rather than a series of discrete letters. Students' precommunicative writing samples can be used as informal assessments of their understanding of the alphabetic principle and knowledge of letter-sound correspondences.

Pre-phonetic stage of spelling development

The pre-phonetic stage is followed by the **semiphonetic stage**. In this stage, a student understands that letters represent sounds. The alphabetic principle may be understood, but letter recognition may not yet be fully developed. In this stage, single letters may be used to represent entire words (e.g., *U* for *you*). Other times, multiple syllables within words may be omitted. Writing produced by students in this stage is still virtually unreadable. Teachers may ask students to provide drawings to supplement their writing to better determine what a student intended to write.

Semiphonetc stage of writing

The third stage in spelling development is the **phonetic stage**. In this stage, students have mastered letter-sound correspondences. Although letters may be written backward or upside down, phonetic spellers are able to write all of the letters in the alphabet. Because phonetic spellers have limited sight vocabulary, irregular words are often spelled incorrectly. However, words that are written may phonetically sound like the spoken word. Additionally, student writing becomes systematic. For example, students are likely to use one letter to represent a digraph or letter blend (e.g., *f* for /ph/).

Phonetic stage of writing

Spelling instruction of common consonant patterns, short vowel sounds, and common affixes or rimes can begin during the phonetic stage. Thus, spelling instruction during the phonetic stage coincides with the instruction of phonics and phonemic awareness that also occurs during this stage of development.

The creation of word walls is advantageous during the phonetic stage of spelling development. On a word wall, words that share common consonant-vowel patterns or letter clusters are written in groups. Students are encouraged to add words to the group. As a result, word walls promote strategic spelling, vocabulary development, common letter combinations, and common morphological units.

The **transitional stage** of spelling occurs when a student has developed a small sight vocabulary and a solid understanding of letter-sound correspondences. Thus, spelling dependence on phonology decreases. Instead, dependence on visual representation and word structure increases. As sight word vocabulary increases during the transition stage, the correct spelling of irregular words will also increase. However, students may still struggle to spell words with long vowel sounds.

Transitional stage of spelling

Differentiation of spelling instruction often begins during the transitional stage. Instruction ought to be guided by data collected through informal observations and informal assessments. Depending on individual needs, lessons may include sight word recognition, morphology, etymology, reading, and writing. It is during the transitional stage that the instruction of homophones can begin. **Homophones** are words that sound the same but have different spellings and meanings (e.g., *their* and *there*). Additionally, students should be expected to begin writing full sentences at the transitional stage. Writing will not only reinforce correct spelling of words but also phonics and vocabulary development.

Conventional spelling is the last and final stage of spelling development. This stage occurs after a student's sight word vocabulary recognition is well developed and the student is able to read fluently and with comprehension. By this stage, students know the basic rules of phonics. They are able to deal with consonants, multiple vowel-consonant blends, homophones, digraphs, and irregular spellings. Due to an increase in sight word recognition at this stage, a conventional speller is able to recognize when a word is spelled incorrectly.

Conventional stage

It is at the conventional spelling stage that spelling instruction can begin to focus on content-specific vocabulary words and words with unusual spellings. In order to further reinforce vocabulary development of such content-specific words and apply phonic skills, students should be encouraged to use the correct spelling of such words within various writing activities.

For even the best conventional spellers, some words will still cause consistent trouble. Students can keep track of words that they consistently spell incorrectly or find confusing in word banks so they can isolate and eventually eliminate their individualized errors. Students can use their word banks as references when they come across a word with which they struggle. Students may also spend time consciously committing the words in their banks to memory through verbal or written practice.

Recognizing Common Orthographic Patterns

As students become more advanced in their decoding abilities, they will begin to read words that are increasingly more complex linguistically. Teachers should continue using decodable text so that students can continue practicing phonics elements and sight words already taught.

Whole-to-part instruction can be used with students who display more advanced decoding abilities. During whole-to-part instruction, a sentence, a word, and then a sound-symbol relationship is the focus of instruction. Additionally, CVCC, CCVC, and CVVC words that contain common and regular letter combinations can be taught as well as regular CVCe words. Teachers can begin introducing less common phonics elements, such as *kn* or *ph*. It is during this stage that students are taught how to add common inflected endings or suffixes (*-ed, -er, -est, -ing,* etc.) to single-syllable base words.

Finally, phonics knowledge is used to spell more complex orthographic patterns in single-syllable words. **Orthography** is the study of a language's spelling conventions. Orthography includes the rules of spelling, hyphenation, capitalization, pronunciation, emphasis, and word breaks. Orthographic processing requires students to use their visual systems to envision, store, recall, and form words. The prescribed teaching sequence of orthographic patterns is found in the next chart.

Orthographic Pattern	Example of Pattern
Awareness of letter-sound correspondences	Understanding that each letter has a certain sound as well as a name
Understanding that letters form words	Recoding certain CVC words like *dog, hug,* and *jar*
Simple consonant blends and matching sound patterns	Recognizing onsets and rimes of single-syllable words like *cat* as *c-at* and *star* as *st-ar*
Recognizing single-syllable words	Uses CVC, CCVC, or CVCC patterns
Ability to read more complex consonant blends	Reading and recognizing single-syllable words like *cross, lamp,* and *track*
Long versus short vowels	Identifying words that contain long and short vowel sounds
Vowel-Vowel and Vowel-Consonant Digraphs	Identifying words like *whey, tree,* and *phone*
Vowel-Vowel Digraphs that have the same sound	Identifying sounds such as /ay/, /ai/, or /a-e/
Vowel-Consonant Digraphs can be associated with different sounds	Identifying words like *cool* versus *boot, harm* versus *hare,* etc.
Complex single-syllable digraphs and trigraphs	Introducing the *tch* trigraph
Syllabication	Ability to split words into syllables
"Silent Letters" within words	Identifying words that contain silent letters such as *write, knock,* or *plumb*
Blending of two-syllable words	Reading two-syllable words such as *stumble, candle,* etc.
Morphemes within two-syllable words	Identifying correct syllabication of two-syllable words like *post-pone* versus *po-stpone*
Meaning of morphemes	An example would be knowing "macro" means "large" or "great"
Understanding letter clusters	Identifying that the "s" at the end of a word means its plural, and that the "ed" at the end of a word means it's in past tense.
Syllabication of nonconventional morphemes with multisyllabic words	Syllabication of morphemes that are not pronounced how they are written, like *ance* or *tion.*

Promoting Reading Comprehension Through Writing Activities

One way to create an effective reader is to practice comprehension through writing activities. While reading should be an active process, writing forces the student to focus more clearly on spelling, sentence combination, punctuation, and other syntax practices that improve one's ability to read a difficult text. A knowledgeable writer is a knowledgeable reader, and students can practice reading through writing the text themselves. Some writing activities that propagate reading comprehension are listed below:

- **Students can Write About the Texts They Read**: One activity in promoting reading comprehension is to have students write about a text after they've read it. This type of writing is called a **response**, where a student will draw conclusions about a text, write about their reactions to the text, or answer questions the instructor has provided relating to the text.

- **Teach Writing Skills in Relation to Reading**: Comprehension can also be improved by teaching students the processes that go into writing a text, such as organizational structure or sentence construction. Teaching spelling and writing vocabulary words also increase reading fluency.

- **Increase the Quantity of Student Writing**: Have students write frequently. Whether it be a response to a text, lesson, or presentation, students should be consistently practicing their writing skills in order to become more familiar with language overall.

Writing Mechanics

Educators must first be masters of the English language in order to teach it. Teachers serve several key roles in the classroom that all require that they know the conventions of grammar, punctuation, and spelling. Teachers are communicators. They must know how to structure their own language for clarity. They must also be able to interpret what the students are saying to accurately either affirm or revise it for correctness. Teachers are educators of language. They are the agents of change from poor-quality conventions to mastery of the concepts. Teachers are responsible for differentiating instruction so that students at all levels and aptitudes can succeed with language learning. Teachers need to be able to isolate gaps in skill sets and decide which skills need intervention in the classroom.

Teachers are evaluators. They are responsible for making key decisions about a student's educational trajectory based on their assessment of the student's capabilities.

Teachers also have great impact on how students view themselves as learners. Teachers are models. They must be superb examples of educated individuals. Just like with any other subject, people need a strong grasp of the basics of language. They will not be able to learn these things unless the teachers themselves have mastered it.

Teachers foster socialization; socialization to cultural norms and to the everyday practices of the community in which they live is of utmost importance to students' lives. These processes begin at home but continue early in a child's life at school. Teachers play a key role in guiding and scaffolding students' socialization skills. If teachers are to excel in this role, they need to be adept with the use of the English language.

Teachers need to have mastery of the conventions of English including:

- Nouns
- Collective Nouns
- Compound Subjects
- Pronouns
- Subjects, Objects, and Compounds
- Pronoun/Noun Agreement
- Indefinite Pronouns
- Choosing Pronouns
- Adjectives
- Compound Adjectives
- Verbs
- Infinitives
- Verb Tenses
- Participles
- Subject/Verb Agreement
- Active/Passive Voice
- Adverbs
- Double Negatives
- Comparisons
- Double Comparisons
- Prepositions
- Prepositional Phrases
- Conjunctions
- Interjections
- Articles
- Types of sentences
- Subjects and Predicates
- Clauses and Phrases
- Pronoun Reference Problems
- Misplaced Modifiers
- Dangling Participial Phrases
- Punctuation
- Periods
- Commas
- Semicolons and Colons
- Parentheses and Dashes
- Quotation Marks
- Apostrophes
- Hyphens
- Question Marks
- Exclamation Points
- Capitalization
- Spelling
- Noun Plurals

- Prefixes and Suffixes
- Spelling Hurdles
- Abbreviations
- Pronunciation
- Homonyms and other easy mix-ups

Writing Development

Like with any complicated processes, writing development begins with the simplest form of indiscernible scribbles and progresses to fully formed words and, finally, to clearly written sentences and paragraphs. This is actually a complicated cognitive process that takes time and instruction to improve.

With very young students, emphasis can focus on simply making letters clear. After all, letters and word formation are the starting blocks of written language. The next phase in development can focus on actually creating words and making sure they are spelled correctly. When students are at the sentence development stage, grammar and linguistic rules become a priority. The foundations of the English language need to be firm in order for students to have good writing. When students have progressed to more advanced levels and are composing fully formed sentences with a specific purpose, it's time to incorporate content-related feedback.

Feedback at all levels of writing development is crucial; this is how students will learn to correct mistakes and strengthen growing skills. Instructor feedback must be clear while also being sensitive to the students' struggles or backgrounds. Differentiated instruction may be required to bolster students' writing skills. A good starting point for overall writing instruction is to introduce students to the stages of writing an original piece.

The goal with the stages of writing is to build on the previous work. The prewriting stage is the time for students to just write down ideas and plan on how they will approach the topic at hand. The actual writing stage then dovetails on this fluidly because the student already has a framework of what the writing will focus on and how they will present information. In addition to practicing physical writing, these stages focus on critical-thinking and planning skills and may lessen the student's stress before they write and receive feedback. Feedback on the initial writing, or first draft, is key. The instructor should be able to assess any difficulties and then steer the student toward improving their writing in the revision stage. After revisions, instructors should examine how effective their feedback was in helping the writing improve overall.

Effective Composing

Good writing is composed of several key elements: development, focus, clarity and coherence, grammatical proficiency, and originality. Different institutions and individual instructors will list such qualities differently, but good composition will have these basic qualities.

Strong compositions have well-developed ideas that are explained clearly throughout the piece. Good writing seems to have been planned and executed without any gaps or confusion. Through their writing, students must essentially develop an idea and line of reasoning that leave readers clear about the focus of the piece. This also means that paragraphs must be arranged in a way that they enhance and expand on the central focus of the paper, using evidence sensibly.

A writer's focus is the central point. A successful composition will not only contain a clear focus but carry the focus throughout the piece. The reader should never lose the focus or be confused by it. The way in which the content is presented throughout the text, while remaining focused on the central idea, is key. This is done by the tactical use of evidence surrounding and supporting claims relating to the central idea.

Language can be elegant and creative, but it must be used in a way the reader can understand. Much of a writer's success will depend on the coherence of the written piece. Paragraphs and the ideas within them should not be random but connect together, seamlessly blending into the next section to advance the focus of the writing. Each paragraph should strengthen the claim. Unnecessary paragraphs disrupt the flow of the writing and distract the reader, ultimately weakening the piece. Naturally, the writing should also be grammatically correct and proofed for accurate spelling and sentence structure.

Originality is the defining aspect of a well-written piece. Students should not parrot the writing style or ideas of others but instead write something that is unique. Ideas, and the way they are presented, should be fresh and approach topics in a way that offers a new perspective to the reader.

Effective Written Expression

Written expression refers to the ability of the writer to fluidly communicate meaning and purpose throughout the composition. Essentially, this refers not only to how clear the central focus of the piece is but how well the ideas surrounding the central focus are presented. If the writer can't successfully express the meaning and implications of the idea, the writing will not be strong.

Effective written expression utilizes detailed, clear communication. A writer doesn't need to unload elaborate diction throughout the paragraphs. Such an embellishment can be distracting to the reader, which actually defeats the principles behind effective writing. Sentences should be direct and emphasize language that, while engaging, remains simple enough for the audience to understand. This doesn't mean abstaining from using advanced words but rather keeping sentences direct and to the point. Students should avoid rambling line after line. Avoiding exaggerating language or overdramatic phrasing is also important. Not only can this confuse the reader, it can also harm the reader's credibility.

A simple formula for effective writing is to introduce an idea, discuss it, and then make a conclusion. This applies for the written piece as a whole but must also be used within individual paragraphs. If a writer just introduces idea after idea with no substance, the reader is left with unsubstantiated claims. Without supporting evidence to understand the view, the reader is left with only opinion. With the implementation of facts and supporting details, this opinion is strengthened. Thus, the reasoning behind the central idea is clearly executed and can be considered seriously. This helps the writer achieve credibility.

Paragraph coherence is vital for effective written expression. Paragraph sequencing and information placement are essential to streamlining the entire piece. Evidence and supporting information should be used to transition from one section to another, up to the conclusion. This enables the information to be clearly expressed. The author should strive to write in a way that, as the piece progresses, the focus becomes clearer and more convincing. By the conclusion of the written piece, the author should also restate his or her thesis to solidify their views and reasoning.

Recursive Steps of the Writing Process

Like with any complicated processes, writing development begins with the simplest form of indiscernible scribbles and progresses to fully formed words and, finally, to clearly written sentences and paragraphs. This is actually a complicated cognitive process that takes time and instruction to improve.

With very young students, emphasis can focus on simply making letters clear. After all, letters and word formation are the starting blocks of written language. The next phase in development can focus on actually creating words and making sure they are spelled correctly. When students are at the sentence development stage, grammar and linguistic rules become a priority. The foundations of the English language need to be firm in order for students to have good writing. When students have progressed to more advanced levels and are composing fully formed sentences with a specific purpose, it's time to incorporate content-related feedback.

Feedback at all levels of writing development is crucial; this is how students will learn to correct mistakes and strengthen growing skills. Instructor feedback must be clear while also being sensitive to the students' struggles or backgrounds. Differentiated instruction may be required to bolster students' writing skills. A good starting point for overall writing instruction is to introduce students to the stages of writing an original piece.

The goal with the stages of writing is to build on the previous work. The prewriting stage is the time for students to just write down ideas and plan on how they will approach the topic at hand. The actual writing stage then dovetails on this fluidly because the student already has a framework of what the writing will focus on and how they will present information. In addition to practicing physical writing, these stages focus on critical-thinking and planning skills and may lessen the student's stress before they write and receive feedback. Feedback on the initial writing, or first draft, is key. The instructor should be able to assess any difficulties and then steer the student toward improving their writing in the revision stage. After revisions, instructors should examine how effective their feedback was in helping the writing improve overall.

Methods of Feedback in the Writing Process

It is almost as important to provide feedback and evaluate a student's skill level as it is to teach. Most classes utilize both formative and summative assessments as a grading template. Although assessment and grading are not the same thing, assessments are often used to award a grade. A *formative assessment* monitors the student's progress in learning and allows continuous feedback throughout the course in the form of homework and in-class assignments, such as quizzes, writing workshops, conferences, or inquiry-based writing prompts. These assessments typically make up a lower percent of the overall grade. Alternatively, a *summative assessment* compares a student's progress in learning against some sort of standard, such as against the progress of other students or by the number of correct answers. These assessments usually make up a higher percent of the overall grade and come in the form of midterm or final exams, papers, or major projects.

One evidence-based method used to assess a student's progress is a rubric. A *rubric* is an evaluation tool that explicitly states the expectations of the assignment and breaks it down into different components. Each component has a clear description and relationship to the assignment as a whole. For writing, rubrics may be *holistic*, judging the overall quality of the writing, or they can be *analytic*, in which different aspects of the writing are evaluated, e.g., structure, style, word choices, and punctuation.

Rubrics can be used in all aspects of a curriculum, including reading comprehension, oral presentations, speeches, performances, papers, projects, and listening comprehension. They are usually formative in nature, but can be summative depending on the purpose. Rubrics allow instructors to provide specific feedback and allow students to understand the expectations for an assignment.

An example of an analytic rubric is displayed below:

Name _____ Date _____

Essay Rubric	4 Mastery	3 Satisfactory	2 Needs Improvement	1 Poor
Writing Quality	-Excellent usage of voice and style -Outstanding organizational skills -Wealth of relevant information	-Style and voice of essay was interesting -Mostly organized -Useful amount of information	-Inconsistent style and voice -Lacked clear organization -Small amount of useful information	-No noticeable style or voice -Virtually no organization -No relevant information
Grammar Conventions	-Essentially no mistakes in grammar -Correct spelling throughout	-Minor amount of grammar and spelling mistakes	-Many errors in grammar conventions and spelling	-Too many grammatical errors to understand the meaning of the piece

Another research-proven strategy is *conferencing*, in which students participate in a group discussion that usually involves the teacher. Students learn best when they can share their thoughts on what they've read or written and receive feedback from their peers and instructors. For writing, conferencing is frequently done in the revision stage. Through discussion, students are also able to enhance their listening and speaking skills. Conferences can be done in a one-on-one setting, typically between a student and instructor, or in a small group of students with guidance from the instructor. They are useful in that they provide an atmosphere of respect where a student can share his or her work and thoughts without fear of judgment. They increase motivation and allow students to explore a variety of topics and discussions. Conferences also allow the instructor to provide immediate feedback or prompt students for deeper explanations of their ideas. The most successful conferences have these characteristics:

- Have a set structure
- Focus on only a few points—too many are confusing or distracting
- Are solution based
- Allow students to both discuss their thoughts/works and receive/provide feedback for others
- Encourage the use of appropriate vocabulary
- Provide motivation and personal satisfaction or pleasure from reading and writing
- Allow a time where questions can be asked and immediately answered

Rubrics and conferencing are both methods that provide useful *feedback*, one of the most important elements in the progress of a student's learning. Feedback is essentially corrective instruction delivered in writing, either verbally or non-verbally. Research has shown that the following techniques are the most effective when giving feedback:

Being Specific

For a student to know exactly how he or she is doing, feedback should be directed towards specific components of a student's writing, listening, or speaking skills, not a holistic overview. For example, writing "Excellent!" on a student's paper or homework is not useful information as it's unclear what was done well. A paper should provide useful comments throughout the body of the work, for example, "Wording is confusing here," or "Great use of adjectives." However, instructor comments should not overwhelm the student's writing; they should be used to focus their attention on specific areas of success or improvement. This encourages the student to keep doing what he or she is doing well and work on what needs improvement without being overwhelmed.

Being Sensitive

Giving feedback is precarious in nature as it entirely depends upon the emotional and mental states of the receiver. Some students do well with "tough love," while others may be discouraged and disheartened to see a slew of comments on their paper. Teachers should pay attention to how a student reacts to feedback. As a general rule, feedback should focus more on the positives so as not to damage self-esteem, while teaching students new techniques for self-correction, instead of simply criticizing what they've done. Also, it's important to try and be aware of the types of feedback each student responds the most effectively to, for example, providing oral feedback for students who don't read well.

Being Prompt

Feedback should be presented sooner rather than later, so that students will not have time to repeat mistakes they are unaware of that may become habitual. Studies have shown that students who are given immediate feedback display a greater increase in performance than those who were given feedback later in the term. As soon as the action has happened, it is important give the appropriate praise or critique so that the student associates the feedback with the action.

Being Explicit

It is important to explain the purpose of the feedback before it is given so that a student does not feel controlled, too closely examined, or competitive. This can cause the learner to feel self-conscious and discourage him or her from performing his or her best. The importance of feedback and how it is meant to improve on a personal skill set should be explained to the student.

Being Focused

Teachers should try and keep the feedback in alignment with the goal the student is expected to achieve. Too much feedback, especially if it is unrelated to the goal, can be overwhelming and distracting from the purpose of the assignment or paper.

Here are some other tips to consider when giving feedback:

- Teachers should be aware of their body language and facial expressions when giving feedback— a frown or grimace can be very discouraging, even if the written feedback was mostly positive.

- It's conducive to concentrate on one thing at a time. If a student submits a paper with a lot of errors, for example, it may be helpful to identify a prevalent pattern of error and work through strategies to correct it so that student does not feel overwhelmed.

- Using effective rubrics can make all the difference—letting students know exactly what is expected will provide them with a basis on which to model their techniques and skills.

- Students should be educated on giving feedback. This can be demonstrated by example and through instruction how to give feedback in a positive, constructive way and correct any behavior that trends toward disrespect or excessive competition. Students should also provide feedback to the teacher as well.

- Teachers should not give the same comments to every student, but make them personal.

- When offering criticism, teachers should always offer tips for how the student can improve.

- It's important to avoid personal comments, e.g., "You're so smart!" or "Math isn't your best subject." Rather, the comments should focus on the writing: e.g., "The organization of this paper is clear."

- Students shouldn't be compared to each other, e.g., "Look how perfectly Victor composed this sentence!" This can galvanize the students into competing with one another.

High-Quality Writing

High-quality writing takes more than simply good writing skills and a knowledge of vocabulary. High-quality writing takes a lot of planning, writing, and revising in order to meet the standards of the audience. Many factors go into high-quality writing, but some major ones, including content, voice, and word choice, are listed below:

Content
The **content** of a piece of writing includes the ideas, structure, language, and effect of a particular text. Content begins with a writer being able to effectively brainstorm and research their topic in order to obtain credibility as an author. Thorough research of a topic and proper citation is the first step in creating good content. Organization of the text is also important to high-quality content, as is knowledge of vocabulary and sentence structure. Finally, good writing content will have an intended effect on the audience, whether that be persuading the audience to act or informing them of how something is done.

Voice
The voice an author selects is also important to note. An author's **voice** is that element of style that indicates their personality. It's important that authors move us as readers; therefore, they will choose a voice that helps them do that. An author's voice may be satirical or authoritative. It may be light-hearted or serious in tone. It may be silly or humorous as well. Voice, as an element of style, can be vague in nature and difficult to identify, since it's also referred to as an author's tone, but it is that element unique to the author. It is the author's "self." A reader can expect an author's voice to vary across literary genres. A non-fiction author will generally employ a more neutral voice than an author of fiction, but use caution when trying to identify voice. Do not confuse an author's voice with a particular character's voice.

Word Choice
An author's choice of words—also referred to as **diction**—helps to convey his or her meaning in a particular way. Through diction, an author can convey a particular tone—e.g., a humorous tone, a serious tone—in order to support the thesis in a meaningful way to the reader.

Connotation is when an author chooses words or phrases that invoke ideas or feelings other than their literal meaning. An example of the use of connotation is the word *cheap*, which suggests something is poor in value or negatively describes a person as reluctant to spend money. When something or someone is described this way, the reader is more inclined to have a particular image or feeling about it or him/her. Thus, connotation can be a very effective language tool in creating emotion and swaying opinion. However, connotations are sometimes hard to pin down because varying emotions can be associated with a word. Generally, though, connotative meanings tend to be fairly consistent within a specific cultural group.

Denotation refers to words or phrases that mean exactly what they say. It is helpful when a writer wants to present hard facts or vocabulary terms with which readers may be unfamiliar. Some examples of denotation are the words *inexpensive* and *frugal*. *Inexpensive* refers to the cost of something, not its value, and *frugal* indicates that a person is conscientiously watching his or her spending. These terms do not elicit the same emotions that *cheap* does.

Authors sometimes choose to use both, but what they choose and when they use it is what critical readers need to differentiate. One method isn't inherently better than the other; however, one may create a better effect, depending upon an author's intent. If, for example, an author's purpose is to inform, to instruct, and to familiarize readers with a difficult subject, his or her use of connotation may be helpful. However, it may also undermine credibility and confuse readers. An author who wants to create a credible, scholarly effect in his or her text would most likely use denotation, which emphasizes literal, factual meaning and examples.

Writing in Various Forms with Different Audiences and Purposes

Determining the Appropriate Mode of Writing

The author's *primary purpose* is defined as the reason an author chooses to write a selection, and it is often dependent on his or her *audience*. A biologist writing a textbook, for example, does so to communicate scientific knowledge to an audience of people who want to study biology. An audience can be as broad as the entire global population or as specific as women fighting for equal rights in the bicycle repair industry. Whatever the audience, it is important that the author considers its demographics—age, gender, culture, language, education level, etc.

If the author's purpose is to persuade or inform, he or she will consider how much the intended audience knows about the subject. For example, if an author is writing on the importance of recycling to anyone who will listen, he or she will use the informative mode—including background information on recycling—and the argumentative mode—evidence for why it works, while also using simple diction so that it is easy for everyone to understand. If, on the other hand, the writer is proposing new methods for recycling using solar energy, the audience is probably already familiar with standard recycling processes and will require less background information, as well as more technical language inherent to the scientific community.

If the author's purpose is to entertain through a story or a poem, he or she will need to consider whom he/she is trying to entertain. If an author is writing a script for a children's cartoon, the plot, language, conflict, characters, and humor would align with the interests of the age demographic of that audience. On the other hand, if an author is trying to entertain adults, he or she may write content not suitable for children. The author's purpose and audience are generally interdependent.

Identifying the Tone, Purpose, and Intended Audience

An author's *writing style*—the way in which words, grammar, punctuation, and sentence fluidity are used—is the most influential element in a piece of writing, and it is dependent on the purpose and the audience for whom it is intended. Together, a writing style and mode of writing form the foundation of a written work, and a good writer will choose the most effective mode and style to convey a message to readers.

Writers should first determine what they are trying to say and then choose the most effective mode of writing to communicate that message. Different writing modes and *word choices* will affect the tone of a piece—that is, its underlying attitude, emotion, or character. The argumentative mode may utilize words that are earnest, angry, passionate, or excited whereas an informative piece may have a sterile, germane, or enthusiastic tone. The tones found in narratives vary greatly, depending on the purpose of the writing. *Tone* will also be affected by the audience—teaching science to children or those who may be uninterested would be most effective with enthusiastic language and exclamation points whereas teaching science to college students may take on a more serious and professional tone, with fewer charged words and punctuation choices that are inherent to academia.

Sentence fluidity—whether sentences are long and rhythmic or short and succinct—also affects a piece of writing as it determines the way in which a piece is read. Children or audiences unfamiliar with a subject do better with short, succinct sentence structures as these break difficult concepts up into shorter points. A period, question mark, or exclamation point is literally a signal for the reader to stop and takes more time to process. Thus, longer, more complex sentences are more appropriate for adults or educated audiences as they can fit more information in between processing time.

The amount of *supporting detail* provided is also tailored to the audience. A text that introduces a new subject to its readers will focus more on broad ideas without going into greater detail whereas a text that focuses on a more specific subject is likely to provide greater detail about the ideas discussed.

Writing styles, like modes, are most effective when tailored to their audiences. Having awareness of an audience's demographic is one of the most crucial aspects of properly communicating an argument, a story, or a set of information.

Choosing the Most Appropriate Type of Writing
Before beginning any writing, it is imperative that a writer have a firm grasp on the message he or she wishes to convey and how he or she wants readers to be affected by the writing. For example, does the author want readers to be more informed about the subject? Does the writer want readers to agree with his or her opinion? Does the writer want readers to get caught up in an exciting narrative? The following steps are a guide to determining the appropriate type of writing for a task, purpose, and audience:

1. Identifying the purpose for writing the piece
2. Determining the audience
3. Adapting the writing mode, word choices, tone, and style to fit the audience and the purpose

It is important to distinguish between a work's purpose and its main idea. The essential difference between the two is that the *main idea* is what the author wants to communicate about the topic at hand whereas the *primary purpose* is why the author is writing in the first place. The primary purpose is what will determine the type of writing an author will choose to utilize, not the main idea, though the two are related. For example, if an author writes an article on the mistreatment of animals in factory farms and, at the end, suggests that people should convert to vegetarianism, the main idea is that vegetarianism would reduce the poor treatment of animals. The primary purpose is to convince the reader to stop eating animals. Since the primary purpose is to galvanize an audience into action, the author would choose the argumentative writing mode.

The next step is to consider to whom the author is appealing as this will determine the type of details to be included, the diction to be used, the tone to be employed, and the sentence structure to be used. An audience can be identified by considering the following questions:

- What is the purpose for writing the piece?
- To whom is it being written?
- What is their age range?
- Are they familiar with the material being presented, or are they just being newly introduced to it?
- Where are they from?
- Is the task at hand in a professional or casual setting?
- Is the task at hand for monetary gain?

These are just a few of the numerous considerations to keep in mind, but the main idea is to become as familiar with the audience as possible. Once the audience has been understood, the author can then adapt the writing style to align with the readers' education and interests. The audience is what determines the *rhetorical appeal* the author will use—ethos, pathos, or logos. *Ethos* is a rhetorical appeal to an audience's ethics and/or morals. Ethos is most often used in argumentative and informative writing modes. *Pathos* is an appeal to the audience's emotions and sympathies, and it is found in argumentative, descriptive, and narrative writing modes. *Logos* is an appeal to the audience's logic and reason and is used primarily in informative texts as well as in supporting details for argumentative pieces. Rhetorical appeals are discussed in depth in the informational texts and rhetoric section of the test.

If the author is trying to encourage global conversion to vegetarianism, he or she may choose to use all three rhetorical appeals to reach varying personality types. Those who are less interested in the welfare of animals but are interested in facts and science would relate more to logos. Animal lovers would relate better to an emotional appeal. In general, the most effective works utilize all three appeals.

Finally, after determining the writing mode and rhetorical appeal, the author will consider word choice, sentence structure, and tone, depending on the purpose and audience. The author may choose words that convey sadness or anger when speaking about animal welfare if writing to persuade, or he or she will stick to dispassionate and matter-of-fact tones, if informing the public on the treatment of animals in factory farms. If the author is writing to a younger or less-educated audience, he or she may choose to shorten and simplify sentence structures and word choice. If appealing to an audience with more expert knowledge on a particular subject, writers will more likely employ a style of longer sentences and more complex vocabulary.

Depending on the task, the author may choose to use a first person, second person, or third person point of view. First person and second person perspectives are inherently more casual in tone, including the author and the reader in the rhetoric, while third person perspectives are often seen in more professional settings.

Evaluating the Effectiveness of a Piece of Writing
An effective and engaging piece of writing will cause the reader to forget about the author entirely. Readers will become so engrossed in the subject, argument, or story at hand that they will almost identify with it, readily adopting beliefs proposed by the author or accepting all elements of the story as believable. On the contrary, poorly written works will cause the reader to be hyperaware of the author, doubting the writer's knowledge of a subject or questioning the validity of a narrative. Persuasive or

expository works that are poorly researched will have this effect, as well as poorly planned stories with significant plot holes. An author must consider the task, purpose, and audience to sculpt a piece of writing effectively.

When evaluating the effectiveness of a piece, the most important thing to consider is how well the purpose is conveyed to the audience through the mode, use of rhetoric, and writing style.

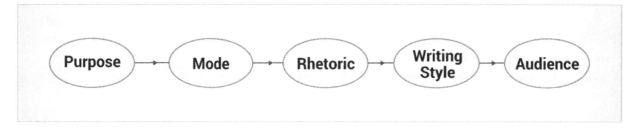

The purpose must pass through these three aspects for effective delivery to the audience. If any elements are not properly considered, the reader will be overly aware of the author, and the message will be lost. The following is a checklist for evaluating the effectiveness of a piece:

- Does the writer choose the appropriate writing mode—argumentative, narrative, descriptive, informative—for his or her purpose?

- Does the writing mode employed contain characteristics inherent to that mode?

- Does the writer consider the personalities/interests/demographics of the intended audience when choosing rhetorical appeals?

- Does the writer use appropriate vocabulary, sentence structure, voice, and tone for the audience demographic?

- Does the author properly establish himself/herself as having authority on the subject, if applicable?

- Does the piece make sense?

Another thing to consider is the medium in which the piece was written. If the medium is a blog, diary, or personal letter, the author may adopt a more casual stance towards the audience. If the piece of writing is a story in a book, a business letter or report, or a published article in a journal or if the task is to gain money or support or to get published, the author may adopt a more formal stance. Ultimately, the writer will want to be very careful in how he or she addresses the reader.

Finally, the effectiveness of a piece can be evaluated by asking how well the purpose was achieved. For example, if students are assigned to read a persuasive essay, instructors can ask whether the author influences students' opinions. Students may be assigned two differing persuasive texts with opposing perspectives and be asked which writer was more convincing. Students can then evaluate what factors contributed to this—for example, whether one author uses more credible supporting facts, appeals more effectively to readers' emotions, presents more believable personal anecdotes, or offers stronger counterargument refutation. Students can then use these evaluations to strengthen their own writing skills.

Reading and Writing as Tools for Inquiry and Research

Sources in Conducting Research

Identifying Relevant Information During Research
Relevant information is that which is pertinent to the topic at hand. Particularly when doing research online, it is easy for students to get overwhelmed with the wealth of information available to them. Before conducting research, then, students need to begin with a clear idea of the question they want to answer.

For example, a student may be interested in learning more about marriage practices in Jane Austen's England. If that student types "marriage" into a search engine, he or she will have to sift through thousands of unrelated sites before finding anything related to that topic. Narrowing down search parameters, then, can aid in locating relevant information.

When using a book, students can consult the table of contents, glossary, or index to discover whether the book contains relevant information before using it as a resource. If the student finds a hefty volume on Jane Austen, he or she can flip to the index in the back, look for the word *marriage* and find out how many page references are listed in the book. If there are few or no references to the subject, it is probably not a relevant or useful source.

In evaluating research articles, students may also consult the title, abstract, and keywords before reading the article in its entirety. Referring to the date of publication will also determine whether the research contains up-to-date discoveries, theories, and ideas about the subject or is outdated.

Evaluating the Credibility of a Print or Digital Source
There are several additional criteria that need to be examined before using a source for a research topic.

The following questions will help determine whether a source is credible:

Author
- o Who is he or she?
- o Does he or she have the appropriate credentials—e.g., M.D, PhD?
- o Is this person authorized to write on the matter through his/her job or personal experiences?
- o Is he or she affiliated with any known credible individuals or organizations?
- o Has he or she written anything else?

Publisher
- o Who published/produced the work? Is it a well-known journal, like National Geographic, or a tabloid, like The National Enquirer?
- o Is the publisher from a scholarly, commercial, or government association?
- o Do they publish works related to specific fields?
- o Have they published other works?
- o If a digital source, what kind of website hosts the text? Does it end in .edu, .org, or .com?

Bias
- o Is the writing objective? Does it contain any loaded or emotional language?
- o Does the publisher/producer have a known bias, such as Fox News or CNN?
- o Does the work include diverse opinions or perspectives?

- o Does the author have any known bias—e.g., Michael Moore, Bill O'Reilly, or the Pope? Is he or she affiliated with any organizations or individuals that may have a known bias—e.g., Citizens United or the National Rifle Association?
  - o Does the magazine, book, journal, or website contain any advertising?

References
  - o Are there any references?
  - o Are the references credible? Do they follow the same criteria as stated above?
  - o Are the references from a related field?

Accuracy/reliability
  - o Has the article, book, or digital source been peer reviewed?
  - o Are all of the conclusions, supporting details, or ideas backed with published evidence?
  - o If a digital source, is it free of grammatical errors, poor spelling, and improper English?
  - o Do other published individuals have similar findings?

Coverage
  - o Are the topic and related material both successfully addressed?
  - o Does the work add new information or theories to those of their sources?
  - o Is the target audience appropriate for the intended purpose?

Research Skills

Classrooms are utilizing more demanding research skills and projects. Science experiments and invention fairs encourage students to develop their own questions and topics to explore through research. Students should select topics that they want to research, apply, and solve. This can then be developed into academic arguments, which counter previous findings on a topic. When evaluating a topic, students can research and explore the topic while using their previous understanding of comparing and contrasting various texts.

With the increased reliance on technology in classrooms, at home, and in all facets of daily life, schools are encouraging the use of technology in lessons. Even in the primary grades, teachers are assigning more research-based projects to introduce technology to students at an early age. This way, when students reach higher grade levels, their previous understanding of how and where to find information to answer questions and summarize information can be developed even further. The older grades incorporate using multiple sources, asking and evaluating questions, and thinking of their own research topics to explore. This development of instructional strategies and research skills proves to be beneficial in the sciences as well as the new generation of S.T.E.M. learning. Again, reading comprehension skills are essential to the development of research skills.

Reference Materials and Media Resources

Multimedia presentations, such as PowerPoint or SlideShare, have been traditionally most effective at the higher education levels. However, as young children are more and more exposed to a world of technology, educators at the primary years are beginning to employ multimedia presentations in the classroom.

If carefully planned out, multimedia presentations can be used to enhance comprehension on virtually any subject. Using powerful graphic imagery that is directly relevant to the topic—coupled with effective textual language or audio—has been particularly effective in a growing number of classrooms.

Presenting students with the challenge of creating their own multimedia presentations can also be very rewarding for educators and students alike. Either independently, in pairs, or in groups, children take the learning process into their own hands with the opportunity to demonstrate the knowledge of a given subject by employing relevant written text and graphics.

Using Technology to Conduct Final Research Products

Teachers are learning to adapt their writing instruction to integrate today's technology standards and to enhance engagement in the writing process. The key is to still build a strong foundation of the fundamentals of writing while using current technology. Gone are the days when writing relied solely on handwritten pieces and when the tools of the trade were pencils, paper, hardback dictionaries, and encyclopedias. Online resources are now the backbone of the writing experience. It is now possible to integrate photo, video, and other interactive components into a completed project to provide a well-rounded engagement with media. In order to have an education conducive to college and career readiness and success, students need online research and digital media writing skills.

There are many compelling reasons to teach students to be digitally aware and prudent users of technology when it comes to their writing. With current digital technology, the writing process has become a much more collaborative experience. In higher education and in career settings, collaborative skills are essential. Publishing and presenting are now simplified such that completed work is often read by a wide variety of audiences. Writing can be instantly shared with parents, peers, educators, and the general public, including experts in the field. Students are more apt to take an interest in the writing process when they know that others are reading their writing. Feedback is also simplified because so many platforms allow comments from readers. Teachers can be interactive with the students throughout the process, allowing formative assessment and integration of personalized instruction. Technology is simply a new vehicle for human connection and interactivity.

Reference Materials and Media Resources

A student may be exposed to a plethora of technology, but this does not mean that she or he necessarily knows how to use it for learning. The teacher is still responsible for guiding, monitoring, and scaffolding the students toward learning objectives. It is critical that educators teach students how to locate credible information and to reliably cite their sources using bibliographies. Platforms and apps for online learning are varied and plentiful. Here are some ideas for how to use technology for writing instruction in the classroom:

- Use a projector with a tablet to display notes and classwork for the group to see. This increases instructional time because notes are already available rather than having to be written in real-time. This also provides the ability to save, email, and post classwork and notes for students and parents to access on their own time. A student can work at his or her own pace and still keep up with instruction. Student screens can be displayed for peer-led teaching and sharing of class work.

- More technology in class means less paperwork. Digital drop-boxes can be used for students to turn in assignments. Teachers can save paper, keep track of student revisions of work, and give feedback electronically.

- Digital media can be used to differentiate instruction for multiple learning styles and multiple skill levels. Instead of using standardized textbook learning for everyone, teachers can create and collect resources for individualizing course content.

- Inquiry- and problem-based learning is easier with increased collaborative capabilities provided by digital tools.

- Digital textbooks and e-readers can replace hardback versions of text that are prone to damage and loss. Students can instantly access definitions for new words, as well as annotate and highlight useful information without ruining a hardbound book.

- Library databases can be used to locate reliable research information and resources. There are digital tools for tracking citation information, allowing annotations for internet content, and for storing internet content.

- Mobile devices may be used in the classroom to encourage reading and writing when students use them to text, post, blog, and tweet.

- PowerPoint and other presentation software can be used to model writing for students and to provide a platform for presenting their work.

- Students can create a classroom blog, review various blog sites, and use blogs as they would diaries or journals. They can even write from the perspective of the character in a book or a famous historical person.

- Web quests can be used to help guide students on research projects. They can get relevant information on specific topics and decide what pieces to include in their writing.

- Students can write about technology as a topic. They can "teach" someone how to use various forms of technology, specific learning platforms, or apps.

- Students can create webpages, make a class webpage, and then use it to help with home-school communication.

- Online feedback and grading systems can be used. There are many to choose from. This may allow students to see the grading rubric and ask questions or receive suggestions from the teacher.

- Students and teachers can use email to exchange ideas with other schools or experts on certain topics that are being studied in the classroom.

- Game show-style reviews can be created for units of study to use on computers or on an overhead projector.

- A wiki website can be created that allows students to collaborate, expand on each other's work, and do peer editing and revision.

- Publishing tools can be used to publish student work on the web or in class newspapers or social media sites.

Practice Questions

1. Which mode of writing aims to inform the reader objectively about a particular subject or idea and typically contains definitions, instructions, or facts within its subject matter?
    a. Argumentative
    b. Informative
    c. Narrative
    d. Descriptive

2. Editorials, letters of recommendation, and cover letters most likely incorporate which writing mode?
    a. Argumentative
    b. Informative
    c. Narrative
    d. Descriptive

3. The type of writing mode an author chooses to use is dependent on which of the following elements?
    a. The audience
    b. The primary purpose
    c. The main idea
    d. Both A and B

4. The rhetorical appeal that elicits an emotional and/or sympathetic response from an audience is known as which of the following?
    a. Logos
    b. Ethos
    c. Pathos
    d. None of the above

5. Which of the following refers to what an author wants to express about a given subject?
    a. Primary purpose
    b. Plot
    c. Main idea
    d. Characterization

6. Which organizational style is used in the following passage?

    There are several reasons why the new student café has not been as successful as expected. One factor is that prices are higher than originally advertised, so many students cannot afford to buy food and beverages there. Also, the café closes rather early; as a result, students go out in town to other late-night gathering places rather than meeting friends at the café on campus.

    a. Cause and effect order
    b. Compare and contrast order
    c. Spatial order
    d. Time order

7. Short, succinct sentences are best written for which of the following audiences?
    a. Adults or people more familiar with a subject
    b. Children or people less familiar a subject
    c. Politicians and academics
    d. University students

8. A student is starting a research assignment on Japanese-American internment camps during World War II, but she is unsure of how to gather relevant resources. Which of the following would be the most helpful advice for the student?
    a. Conduct a broad internet search to get a wide view of the subject.
    b. Consult an American history textbook.
    c. Find websites about Japanese culture such as fashion and politics.
    d. Locate texts in the library related to World War II in America and look for references to internment camps in the index.

9. Which of the following should be evaluated to ensure the credibility of a source?
    a. The publisher, the author, and the references
    b. The subject, the title, and the audience
    c. The organization, stylistic choices, and transition words
    d. The length, the tone, and the contributions of multiple authors

10. Which of the following is true of using citations in a research paper?
    a. If a source is cited in the bibliography, it is not necessary to cite it in the paper as well.
    b. In-text citations differ in format from bibliographic citations.
    c. Students should learn one standard method of citing sources.
    d. Books and articles need to be cited, but not websites or multimedia sources.

11. Which of the following is true regarding the integration of source material to maintain the flow of ideas in a research project or paper?
    a. There should be at least one quotation or paraphrase in every paragraph.
    b. If a source is paraphrased instead of being directly quoted, it is not necessary to include a citation.
    c. An author's full name must be used in every signal phrase.
    d. In-text citations should be used to support the paper's argument without overwhelming the student's writing.

12. Which citation style requires the inclusion of the author's last name, the title of the book or article, and its publication date in a bibliography entry?
    a. MLA
    b. APA
    c. Chicago
    d. All of the above

13. Which of the following qualities are necessary for effective speech delivery?
    a. Knowledge, erudite vocabulary, and conviction
    b. Charm, wit, and connection
    c. Confidence, authenticity, and succinctness
    d. Compassion, empathy, and tolerance

14. Which of the following components are advantageous and disadvantageous regarding the use of Microsoft PowerPoint presentations?

    a. They present information that can be taken home and reviewed later, but the audience may choose to read rather than listen.

    b. They allow the audience to follow along with the process of explaining difficult concepts and copy down their own version, but there is limited space that may need to be erased.

    c. They allow for pictures, words, and videos, but they can be distracting from the presence of the speaker.

    d. They allow for participants to interact with the physical world which helps solidify concepts, but they can be distracting if not properly introduced.

15. Which of the following should be considered before utilizing a technological device in the classroom?

    a. The age of the students

    b. Whether it is user friendly

    c. If it will be used in the real world

    d. All of the above

16. Which of the following refers to a teaching strategy in which two or more students work together to develop a project, work through an idea, or solve a problem?

    a. Listening

    b. Collaborative learning

    c. Active learning

    d. Discussion

17. A method of learning in which the student learns through physical interaction with an object is referred to as which of the following?

    a. Auditory Learning

    b. Visual Learning

    c. Kinesthetic Learning

    d. Distance Learning

18. Which of the following defines the stage of writing that involves adding to, removing, rearranging, or re-writing sections of a piece?

    a. The revising stage

    b. The publishing stage

    c. The writing stage

    d. The pre-writing stage

19. A research-proven approach to teaching writing that involves a short lesson, independent writing time, and sharing is known as which of the below?

    a. Writing workshop

    b. Teacher modeling

    c. The writer's notebook

    d. Freewriting

20. Which of the following is true regarding the most effective methods of teaching the writing process?
    a. Instruction should be standardized so that all students should learn writing in the same way.
    b. Feedback should be generalized, giving overall instruction for improvement instead of focusing on certain aspects of writing.
    c. The most important way a student learns is by doing, so they should be given as many opportunities to write as possible.
    d. Students should be compared to one another, so lower-achieving students can model their writing skills on those of more proficient students.

21. Which of the following is true of assessing student writing?
    a. Students should only be given positive feedback so as not to make them feel discouraged.
    b. Students should engage in peer assessments without instructor interference, to increase independent writing skills.
    c. Writing assessments should always be holistic so students get the "big picture" of effective writing.
    d. Writing assessments should be returned in a timely manner.

22. Which of the following is an evaluation tool that explicitly states the expectations of an assignment and breaks it down into components and evaluation criteria?
    a. A one-on-one conference
    b. An analytic rubric
    c. A verbal feedback session
    d. A discussion with peers

23. When it comes to class discussions, setting guidelines for the discussion, preventing distracting tangents, and refraining from arguing with students are examples of which of the following?
    a. Cultivating an environment of inclusion and mutual respect
    b. Keeping discussions productive
    c. Encouraging participation
    d. Ensuring accountability

24. If student participation in discussion is low, which of the following should be done to encourage more active participation?
    a. Divide the classroom into smaller groups so that shy students will feel more comfortable speaking up.
    b. Brainstorm ideas related to the topic on the board.
    c. Allow students to lead discussion or suggest topics.
    d. All of the above

Answer Explanations

1. B: The key word here is "inform," which is the primary purpose of all informative modes. They contain facts, definitions, instructions, and other elements with the objective purpose of informing a reader—such as study guides, instruction manuals, and textbooks. Choice *A* is incorrect because an argumentative mode contains language that is subjective and is intended to persuade or to inform with a persuasive bias. Choice *C* is incorrect as a narrative mode is used primarily to tell a story and has no intention of informing, nor is the language inherently objective. Choice *D* is incorrect as descriptive modes possess no inherent intent to inform, and are used primarily to describe.

2. A: Editorials, recommendation letters, and cover letters all seek to persuade a reader to agree with the author, which reflects an argumentative mode. Choice *B* is incorrect because the intent of the above examples is to persuade a reader to agree with the author, not to present information. Choice *C* is incorrect as the above examples are not trying to tell a story. Choice *D* is also incorrect because while the above examples may contain many descriptions, that is not their primary purpose.

3. D: Both the audience and primary purpose are important for choosing a writing mode. The audience is an important factor as the diction, tone, and stylistic choices of a written piece are tailored to fit the audience demographic. The primary purpose is the reason for writing the piece, so the mode of writing must be tailored to the most effective delivery method for the message. Choice *A* is incorrect because it only takes into account one of the aspects for choosing a mode and the audience, but leaves out the primary purpose. Choice *B* is incorrect for the same reason, except it only takes into account the primary purpose and forgets the audience. Choice *C* is incorrect as the main idea is the central theme or topic of the piece, which can be expressed in any form the author chooses. Because the mode depends on the reason the author wrote the piece, the main idea is not an important factor in determining which mode of writing to use.

4. C: Pathos is the rhetorical appeal that draws on an audience's emotions and sympathies. Choice *A* is incorrect as logos appeals to the audience's logic, reason, and rational thinking, using facts and definitions. Choice *B* is incorrect because ethos appeals to the audience's sense of ethics and moral obligations. Choice *D* is incorrect because *C* contains the correct answer; thus, the answer cannot be "None of the above."

5. C: The main idea of a piece is its central theme or subject and what the author wants readers to know or understand after they read. Choice *A* is incorrect because the primary purpose is the reason that a piece was written, and while the main idea is an important part of the primary purpose, the above elements are not developed with that intent. Choice *B* is incorrect because while the plot refers to the events that occur in a narrative, organization, tone, and supporting details are not used only to develop plot. Choice *D* is incorrect because characterization is the description of a person.

6. A: The passage describes a situation and then explains the causes that led to it. Also, it utilizes cause and effect signal words, such as *causes, factors, so,* and *as a result. B* is incorrect because a compare and contrast order considers the similarities and differences of two or more things. *C* is incorrect because spatial order describes where things are located in relation to each other. Finally, *D* is incorrect because time order describes when things occurred chronologically.

7. B: Children and less educated audiences tend to understand short, succinct sentences more effectively because their use helps increase information processing. Choice *A* is incorrect as longer, more fluid sentences are best used for adults and more educated audiences because they minimize processing times and allow for more information to be conveyed. Choices *C* and *D* are incorrect because there is no correlation between a given profession and a writing style; rather, it depends on how familiar the audience is with a given subject.

8. D: Relevant information refers to information that is closely related to the subject being researched. Students might get overwhelmed by information when they first begin researching, so they should learn how to narrow down search terms for their field of study. Both Choices *A* and *B* are incorrect because they start with a range that is far too wide; the student will spend too much time sifting through unrelated information to gather only a few related facts. Choice *C* introduces a more limited range, but it is not closely related to the topic that is being researched. Finally, Choice *D* is correct because the student is choosing books that are more closely related to the topic and is using the index or table of contents to evaluate whether the source contains the necessary information.

9. A: The publisher, author, and references are elements of a resource that determine credibility. If the publisher has published more than one work, the author has written more than one piece on the subject, or the work references other recognized research, the credibility of a source will be stronger. Choice *B* is incorrect because the subject and title may be used to determine relevancy, not credibility, and the audience does not have much to do with the credibility of a source. Choice *C* is incorrect because the organization, stylistic choices, and transition words are all components of an effectively-written piece, but they have less to do with credibility, other than to ensure that the author knows how to write. The length and tone of a piece are a matter of author's preference, and a work does not have to be written by multiple people to be considered a credible source.

10. B: In-text citations are much shorter and usually only include the author's last name, page numbers being referenced, and for some styles, the publication year. Bibliographic citations contain much more detailed reference information. *B* is incorrect because citations are necessary both in the text and in a bibliography. *C* is incorrect because there are several different citation styles depending on the type of paper or article being written. Rather, students should learn when it is appropriate to apply each different style. *D* is incorrect because all sources need to be cited regardless of medium.

11. D: The purpose of integrating research is to add support and credibility to the student's ideas, not to replace the student's own ideas altogether. Choice *A* is incorrect as the bulk of the paper or project should be comprised of the author's own words, and quotations and paraphrases should be used to support them. Outside sources should be included when they enhance the writer's argument, but they are not required in every single paragraph. Choice *B* is also incorrect because regardless of whether ideas are directly quoted or paraphrased, it is essential to always credit authors for their ideas. The use of the author's full name in every signal phrase is unnecessary, so Choice *C* is also incorrect.

12. D: Although there are differences between each formatting style, they all include the same basic components listed in the question for bibliography entries—the author's name, the title of the work, and its publication date. Therefore, the correct answer is all of the above.

13. C: Confidence, authenticity, and succinctness are the most important aspects of speech delivery as they instill trust in the audience and deliver a message succinctly, which reduces the likelihood that the audience's attention will wander. Choice *A* is incorrect as knowledge is important for a good speech, as is conviction, but appropriate vocabulary depends on the audience. The message could get lost if vocabulary is inappropriate or unfamiliar to the audience. Choice *B* is incorrect because though charm, wit, and connection could be useful, charming people may also be perceived as inauthentic and lose credibility with their audience. Choice *D* is incorrect because though compassion, empathy, and tolerance are all good qualities in a person and work well in certain speech topics, they are not inherent qualities that one must possess to deliver a good speech.

14. C: Microsoft PowerPoint is the medium that can present pictures, words, and videos because of its inherent digital format, but the vastness of the projection and presence of information can distract an audience from the presence of the speaker. Choice *A* is incorrect because handouts are print mediums that present information that can be taken home and reviewed later, and participants can choose to read rather than listen. Choice *B* is incorrect because blackboards, whiteboards, and overhead projectors allow for students to follow along with processes, but provide limited space. Choice *D* is incorrect because physical objects allow for participants to interact with the physical world, but they can be distracting if not properly introduced.

15. D: The age of the students is an important aspect to consider when using technology because many devices have basic requirements for motor and comprehension skills. User friendliness is important as not all students have the same amount of technological literacy. Teaching students to use a device that they will never use again is futile, so it's more practical to use technology that they will use in the real world. Choice *D* is the correct answer because it includes all of these aspects; Choices *A*, *B*, and *C* are incorrect because they only include one of the above aspects.

16. B: Collaborative learning is defined as a teaching strategy is which two or more students work together to learn something new. Choice *A* is incorrect because listening is not a teaching strategy so much as a learning strategy, and listening is required for most types of learning. Choice *C* is incorrect because active learning is when a student learns by doing, either by teaching another student or writing a summary. Two or more students coming together to learn actively, as opposed to one instructing the other, is more indicative of collaborative learning. Choice *D* is incorrect because although discussions may occur with two or more students, it does not usually include any form of active learning, such as creating a project or solving a problem.

17. C: One component of kinesthetic learning is students learning through physical interaction with something, such as a model or an interactive computer simulation. Choice *A* is incorrect as auditory learning is when a student learns through listening, such as listening to a lecture on a podcast. Choice *B* is incorrect because visual learning occurs when a student learns through watching or observing, such as an instructional video. Choice *D* is incorrect because distance learning occurs when the teacher and student are not in the same place and is achieved through technological means.

18. A: The revising stage involves adding, removing, and rearranging sections of a written work. Choice *B* is incorrect as the publishing stage involves the distribution of the finished product to the publisher, teacher, or reader. Choice *C* is incorrect because the writing stage is the actual act of writing the work, and generally does not including editing or revision. Choice *D* is incorrect as the pre-writing stage involves the planning, drafting, and researching of the intended piece.

19. A: The writing workshop is the teaching strategy involving a short lesson on how to write or to give the topic, an individual writing session, and then a sharing section in which the students read what they have written and listens to others. Choice *B* is incorrect because teacher modeling means being an example from which the students can imitate their writing and behavior. It requires that teachers be skilled writers themselves. Choice *C* is incorrect because the writer's notebook is the physical or digital notebook where students write and store their work. And Choice *D* is incorrect because freewriting refers to giving students a set length of time to write on a subject without editing their ideas or expressions.

20. C: Giving the students many opportunities to write is the most effective way they learn to write, and the most effective learning occurs through doing. Choice *A* is incorrect because instruction should not be standardized; it should be individualized to fit different students' needs. Choice *B* is incorrect because feedback should be specific, not generalized, so that a student may focus on the parts of his or her writing that need work, while also recognizing what he or she is doing well in other areas. Choice *D* is incorrect because though it can be helpful for students to evaluate and discuss each other's work, it is important to avoid creating a culture of comparison and competition in the classroom, which can lead to lower morale and negatively affect relationships between students.

21. D: Writing assessments should be conducted and returned in a timely manner so that students can learn from their mistakes, which in turn helps them to avoid repeating the same errors and developing ineffective writing habits. Choice *A* is incorrect because though it is important to present criticism in a constructive and encouraging way, it is better to integrate positive feedback with suggestions for improvement. Choice *B* is incorrect because peer review can be an effective learning tool, but only when it is properly modeled and monitored by the instructor. Choice *C* is incorrect because, although a holistic approach is one way to approach writing assessments, it is not the only useful method; in some cases, students need to focus on one specific area of improvement.

22. B: An analytic rubric is an evaluation tool that explicitly states the expectations of an assignment and breaks it down into components. Choice *A* is incorrect because a conference is a discussion, not a tool. Choice *C* is incorrect because although verbal feedback may accompany a completed rubric, it is not the tool itself. Choice *D* is incorrect because a discussion with peers is not a tool, though it may incorporate evaluation.

23. B: Keeping discussions productive means that the instructor guides the flow of discussion to ensure adherence to the topic, which would entail preventing tangents and not engaging with the student should they wish to argue. Choice *A* is incorrect because cultivating an environment of inclusion and mutual respect involves letting everyone have a chance to speak, monitoring student behavior for respect and tolerance, and educating students on cultural differences. Choice *C* is incorrect because encouraging participation involves galvanizing the students by calling on them, writing their responses on the board, or having them create their own topic. Choice *D* is incorrect because ensuring accountability requires that students prepare for class participation by doing homework or taking quizzes, etc. and are held accountable by being assigned or deducted points.

24. D: Dividing students into smaller groups allows for shy students who are intimidated by a large group of people to feel more comfortable in participating. Allowing students to lead discussion or suggest topics gives them more responsibility while also encouraging them to prepare more for class and letting them choose topics that they are interested in. Brainstorming ideas together can give students a starting point when they do not feel confident or knowledgeable about speaking up on a topic. Therefore, *D*—all of the above—is the best answer.

Constructed Response

Constructed Response 1

Prepare an Organized Written Response to a Topic Relating to the Development of Student Literacy.

Scenario: Mr. Brown is a reading specialist at Carroll High School and assists several teachers and classes with literacy development skills. While most students seem to be writing well, Mr. Brown notices that several students in the classes seem to have trouble reading written words. These children come from a wide range of backgrounds, including native and non-native English speakers.

Task 1: What are some ways Mr. Brown can assess the students' skill levels to determine where the root of their reading issues lie?

Task 2: Describe how Mr. Brown can guide the instructors in addressing the reading issues with differentiated instruction.

Constructed Response 2

Prepare an Organized Written Response to a Case Study of an Elementary Student.

Scenario: The following case study is focused on Caleb, a second-grade student. Caleb's primary instructor has noticed that when Caleb reads material aloud in class, he will often take long pauses and read the sentences slower than the other students. This sometimes causes him to stutter or hesitate during longer sentences. Another issue is that sometimes he will switch the order of the words he sees, for example, putting the word *the* after the word *cat* in a sentence. Despite this, Caleb is very bright and seems to fully grasp the context of the material. He also appears to be engaged when answering questions but is hesitant when having to read in front of the class. Caleb's teacher has requested that Mr. Breiner, the reading specialist, evaluate Caleb to understand what might be causing his issues. While Caleb is highly intelligent, the teacher is wondering whether his problems with reading may indicate a reading disorder. Whatever is delaying Caleb's reading, Mr. Breiner has been requested to present ideas on how to help Caleb's reading skills improve. The teacher wants to be able to learn how to address reading issues like Caleb's in the future, or at least be able to identify core literary issues very early in the developmental stage.

Using the information in the scenario and the document below, write a response in which you apply your knowledge of literacy assessment and instructional strategies to analyze this case study. Your response should completely address the following tasks:

Teacher notes:

- When reading the sentence, "The next-door neighbors adopted the cat that had been homeless," Caleb switched *the* and *cat*. He also seemed to take longer to sound out *homeless*.

- Longer sentences seem to cause Caleb confusion when reading aloud.

- In some of his writing responses, Caleb will sometimes switch the letters within the words or the words themselves.

- Caleb understands material clearly and gives insightful thoughts aloud. No speech problems were observed.

Task 1: Identify methods of observation that may indicate whether or not Caleb has a learning disorder. What kind of assessments can be used to determine if his reading difficulties are tied to specific written English structures or if his pausing indicates other psychological disconnects?

Task 2: Based on Caleb's reading difficulties, what are some teaching strategies that can be used to help him improve? Provide details on why differentiating Caleb's instruction would be a major step in bolstering his reading ability.

Constructed Response 3

Prepare an Organized Written Response to Instruct Teachers on What Process to Use.

Scenario: The teachers in an elementary school are proactively trying to implement content-area reading instruction in their classrooms. Their goal is to better their students' writing skills and increase comprehension and writing fluency. However, their budget is low, and the implementation must be cost-effective.

Task 1: Briefly provide an example of content-area reading instruction and describe the process in full detail while aligning the process with the budget constraints.

Task 2: Talk about how this instruction will align with an increase in comprehension and writing fluency for the entire school.

Dear Praxis Teaching Reading Test Taker,

We would like to start by thanking you for purchasing this study guide. We hope that we exceeded your expectations.

Our goal in creating this study guide was to cover all of the topics that you will see on the test. We also strove to make our practice questions as similar as possible to what you will encounter on test day. With that being said, if you found something that you feel was not up to your standards, please send us an email and let us know.

We would also like to let you know about other books in our catalog that may interest you, all of which can be found on Amazon.

Praxis Elementary Education Multiple Subjects Exam

amzn.com/1628454326

Praxis English Language Arts Content Knowledge Exam

amzn.com/1628454105

Praxis General Science Content Knowledge Exam

amzn.com/1628455632

Praxis Mathematics Content Knowledge Exam

amzn.com/1628455624

Praxis Social Studies Content Knowledge Exam

amzn.com/1628454210

We have study guides in a wide variety of fields. If the one you are looking for isn't listed above, then try searching for it on Amazon or send us an email.

Thanks Again and Happy Testing!
Product Development Team
info@studyguideteam.com

Interested in buying more than 10 copies of our product? Contact us about bulk discounts:

bulkorders@studyguideteam.com

FREE Test Taking Tips DVD Offer

To help us better serve you, we have developed a Test Taking Tips DVD that we would like to give you for FREE. **This DVD covers world-class test taking tips that you can use to be even more successful when you are taking your test.**

All that we ask is that you email us your feedback about your study guide. Please let us know what you thought about it – whether that is good, bad or indifferent.

To get your **FREE Test Taking Tips DVD**, email freedvd@studyguideteam.com with "FREE DVD" in the subject line and the following information in the body of the email:

  a. The title of your study guide.

  b. Your product rating on a scale of 1-5, with 5 being the highest rating.

  c. Your feedback about the study guide. What did you think of it?

  d. Your full name and shipping address to send your free DVD.

If you have any questions or concerns, please don't hesitate to contact us at freedvd@studyguideteam.com.

Thanks again!

Made in the USA
Monee, IL
29 April 2020